STUDENTS

As

TEACHERS...

THINGS THEY TAUGHT ME;
LIFE LESSONS THEY GAVE ME

Lessons of Inspiration, Dedication, Caring, Motivation,
Purpose...Lessons of Life

by
David Gregory

"Through stories shared with wit and grace from his lifetime career as a Music Educator/Band Director, David Gregory reaffirms for music educators of all ages the importance of our chosen profession."
—Dr. Mary Schneider, Director of Bands, Eastern Michigan University

"The power and impact of these stories is so meaningful and deep-seated that they are important not only to band directors and teachers, but to people in every walk of life. I found the book to be totally captivating with wonderful, poignant stories. Additionally, I was intrigued by the writing style which had a way of keeping the reader wanting to continue for more insights."
—Hal J. Gibson, Colonel US Army (Ret)/Conductor Emeritus United States Army Field Band.

"Dr. Gregory offers a review of the many experiences that have catapulted him to the forefront of the profession focusing on the ultimate WHY of the WHAT and HOW of our vocational pathways. He reaches beyond the pedagogical blueprint and spotlights the REALITY of the band directing community and the immeasurable benefits of banding together."
—Tim Lautzenheiser, Founder-Attitude Concepts for Today

<u>Special Thanks</u>

A very special "Thank You" to so many who helped make this book a reality.

To my wife Cheryl, whom I met on a blind date in the ninth grade and with whom I have been enchanted since, no words can appropriately express my gratitude for our life together and the love we have shared. Day by day...

To my family, you have been my anchor throughout my career. You have supported me and guided me in directions I should go. Many are not so fortunate.

To my colleagues and friends, you have given me so much and allowed me to do many wonderful things during my career. I am forever grateful to you.

And...

To my students...the thousands who passed through my life and career, each leaving your imprint... you were, and are, the source of countless moments of joy, wonderful memories, many challenges, and countless lessons taught. You will always be the most cherished reward of my teaching career. Thank you for teaching me while you were my student. I will forever be indebted to you for all you gave me and all you did to make my life richer. Thank you, my young scholars.

Dedication

With sincere appreciation and profound gratitude this book of "Lessons" is dedicated to:

<u>Colonel Hal J. Gibson</u>...My friend of many years, my mentor, role model, icon of our profession, and a person who cares deeply for our art form. One who always found ways to help and encourage those most in need. He did that for me when he least thought.

and to:

<u>Dr. William J. Moody</u>...My teacher, mentor, and friend. The one who moved me toward "Unaccustomed Earth."

I owe much to you both.

Foreword

The following stories are life lessons taught to me by students. My career of more than five decades was spent teaching music, more specifically, band. I was a band director, which placed me in the enviable position of having students return to my classroom for several years, not for just one.

The life lessons I learned from my students are exactly that...lessons that can stand one in good stead through life's journey. But more importantly, these lessons can serve to encourage, inspire, teach, and guide... to help give hope to other teachers as they attempt to navigate the stressful and demanding classrooms of the 21st century. They are, among others, lessons of perseverance, loss, commitment, humor, beauty, and discovery.

It is my hope the readers, in whatever the profession or environment they find themselves, will take the opportunity to read and reflect on the messages of these stories. Every effort was made to ensure student anonymity as it was my belief their stories were best told without identification while their messages were kept intact.

I truly believe there are lessons for all embedded in the "**Things my students taught me... life lessons they gave me.**"

Contents

Introduction

I am a teacher. Teaching is my calling. More specifically, I am a band director.

For over a half century some of the greatest rewards in my life came from helping my students. Serving as their teacher gave me opportunities to help guide them, counsel them, serve as a role model for them, share my love of teaching with them, watch them grow into who they would become...and to learn from them.

Only after a career filled with teaching students when I had reached the "evening of my professional day," did I truly realize how much my students had taught me, how many incredible lessons of life they had shared with me, and how "splendid the day had been." The following stories, presented from the perspective of a band director who conducted junior high, high school, college/university, adult, and professional ensembles during his career, are only some of the inspiring, beautiful, funny, tragic, and poignant lessons they taught me...while I was their teacher.

Each of us is a teacher and each is a student...we learn as both.

"One must wait until the evening to see how splendid the day has been."

— Sophocles

The Provenance of the Rose

The State of Grace Grandiflora rose was planted by the Grandmother in her later years as a source of pleasure in her garden. It flourished and grew and produced hundreds of magnificent blooms each year. Some years later the Mother was given this beautiful plant to take with her when the Grandmother moved into her assisted living home. The Grandmother wanted to pass along to the Mother something that had been special in her home...a way to share the beauty.

The plant continued to produce fragrant flowers in its new location and brought delight to all who visited. The Mother, and her Daughter, continued to enjoy the rich fragrance and magnificent colors...things that were meaningful because they had been part of the lives of family members before them. This flower was part of a legacy.

Eventually both moved from that home and left the rose bush behind. Another family moved in, but the care given the plant was not the same as that of the previous owners. Not many years passed until another family lived in the house, then another. The rose bush was not tended nor valued as it had been in years past, but somehow it survived and continued to bring beauty into the lives of those who came into contact with it. That was its purpose.

All who lived and visited in that home enjoyed the beauty and fragrance of the State of Grace Grandiflora rose. Most never knew how it got there, who cared for it, to whom it had belonged over the years, or why it was there. They simply enjoyed something beautiful that had begun long ago by someone...something that was passed from person to person to person, each having their lives enriched by something done by someone else. The simple beauty of the rose gave much to many...without expectations of return.

The beauty of the rose continued to give to others long after it was planted. Such was its purpose; such was its nature. A lesson for all...each of us has a provenance.

PART ONE:
LESSONS IN STORIES

Chapter One:
The Lesson of Belonging

The Tuba Player

"I had come to a place where I was meant to be."
— *Pat Conroy,* ***The Lords of Discipline***

He was a quiet kid from the poor side of town. He lived in "The Projects," as that part of town was called, but at the beginning of his junior year in high school had been reassigned from his neighborhood school to mine for the purpose of achieving racial balance in our school system as required by law at that time. He was a tuba player, mainly because his parents could not afford to buy him an instrument but the school had provided one.

His demonstrated musical proficiency was average, but his interest level was significant. Possibly his quiet nature was, at least in part, because he was in a new and completely different environment...one not of his choosing. He was now in the racial minority of the student population where at his previous school he had been in the majority. Whatever the circumstances, he was a quiet and polite and hard-working student who seemed to enjoy being in the band.

He very seldom if ever missed school and he was absent even fewer times from marching band practice. As his first year in my band progressed, he became more involved with fellow band members, both socially and musically and as a result, his musical abilities improved dramatically. He became more outgoing as he made several friends in the band, and he seemed to enjoy spending more time in the band room outside of rehearsal obligations. It seemed to be a comfortable and welcoming place for him. He appeared to have found people with whom he shared common goals of musical and personal excellence.

Sometime during late fall of his senior year in our band he came by my office one day during his lunch break and asked if I had a minute to talk. He knew my door was always open, both figuratively and literally, but he wanted to make certain this "drop by" was more than just that. He came in and sat down across from my desk and seemed to be considering how to put his thoughts into words. Finally he said, "Mr. Gregory, you know, when I put on our marching band uniform and go on the field for our halftime and contest shows, I'm just like our first trumpet player."

I jokingly said to him, "That's not true. You're Black and he's White. You're tall and he's short. You never have the melody and he always plays the melody. He's made all-state band and I have to push you to get you to learn your major scales. And you and I don't have any money and his family is rich." We laughed together, but he sat quietly for a few seconds and then said, "Yeah, except not everybody knows that stuff. But when we put on our band uniforms and go out on the football field and do all those great things together, I'm just like him. Nobody can tell us apart because we all look the same." Lesson taught; lesson learned.

As the years passed, the profound implications and the power of his message have stayed with me and have reminded me that even while I was his band director, he was "teaching me" to understand the significance of the lesson of belonging. Possibly too often we as directors think more of "what the student can do for the band" than "what the band can do for the student."

Nearly 50 years later at a band reunion entitled "One More Time" (no idea where the organizers came up with that theme...), hundreds of former students gathered to remember and celebrate our times together. During the comments and remembrances portion of the event, the tuba player took the opportunity to speak to his friends about his time in our band and how much it meant to him and the impact it had on his life. He told everyone that the band and his band director were the reasons he finished high school rather than dropping out and getting a not-so-good job. Instead, his life path took him to a successful military career and successful business ventures in the years after his high school band time.

Reminder

Each of us very likely has "The Tuba Player" in our classroom at some time...maybe playing a different instrument, maybe even in a class other than band. Possibly that person is just another person in our life we have not yet taken the time to see. A tenet of our teaching lives should be: "Through our work we help change the lives of our students." There will be many who wish to "be just like the first trumpet player."

The French Horn Player

"What is belonging?" we ask. She says, "Where loneliness ends."
— *Rivers Solomon, **The Deep***

She was a good French horn player, not quite "all-state good," but a very good section leader. She was smart, perceptive, musical, and smiled easily. But there was something about her that seemed private, almost bashful. She never missed band rehearsals and was always early. In fact, she seemed to enjoy staying around after rehearsal and visiting with other band members, especially for after-school practices.

Sometime during the first part of her senior year her personality began to change. She was quieter, less engaging, and less willing to take the lead as the principal French horn player in our symphonic band. Even her participation in marching band appeared to be less confident and more tentative. I would ask her from time to time how things were going with her schoolwork as she always did well with her band assignments. She would say things were "OK," but it seemed as if her "OK" was somewhat conditional.

Around mid-October of that year a friend, who was also a band director in the same school system, mentioned to me while we were visiting one evening that he had learned my French horn player's parents were putting a great deal of pressure on her because of her time spent with band activities. He said the father in particular was upset with me because his daughter was so involved with something he felt was "a waste of her time." He wanted her to follow **his** plan for her career and life rather than the path she might choose. Consequently, he was putting pressure on his daughter to drop band, or at least to spend less time being involved with it.

He complained about having to have the marching band uniform cleaned regularly, as per the handbook agreement he had signed at the beginning of the year. He became angry with his daughter because she told him how much she enjoyed being part of something so meaningful as the band. He threatened to come onto the field where our marching band was practicing and physically remove her if we ever ran overtime in ending rehearsal.

When he came to my office to turn in the receipt for having the marching uniform cleaned (he insisted on bringing the receipt rather than allowing his daughter to turn it in as was the standard practice), he inevitably would embarrass his daughter through his words and actions toward me. He would habitually be late picking her up from evening band events such as football games and concerts and he would not allow her to have a car. Many times she would be the last one waiting for her ride home late after the band returned from a football game. He did not like what we were doing with our band activities and said publicly he thought they were a waste of her time. As a result she became more withdrawn from her friends and more passive in her approach to her work. She seemed confused...lost.

Sometime in the early winter months, probably late January, I received a phone call at home one Friday evening. It was the father of my French horn player. He apologized for calling me at home, especially on a weekend evening, said he was embarrassed by his behavior toward me and the band, and offered an apology. Apology accepted, but there was no need. My interest was in my students and what was best for them. Sensing something very serious had taken place, I asked if I could be of assistance. He hesitated then explained what had happened. His daughter had run away from home and he had no idea where she might be. He and his wife were grief-stricken and paralyzed with fear and did not know what to do.

Quietly he told me the circumstances leading up to this breaking point, explaining that he and his wife had planned the careers of each of their children and music was not a part of any of them. He acknowledged he was the reason his daughter had run away. She kept saying to him that being in the band was the thing she enjoyed most in her life. It was the place where she felt she belonged and a place where she believed she could make a difference. It brought joy to her life.

He further said to me he finally realized how much being part of our band meant to his daughter as it possibly was the most important part of her life at that time, and admitted he was grossly negligent in depriving her of that enjoyment during her teenage years. His final comments were these, "I just want to know if she's safe. I know she won't contact me but I think if she reaches out to anyone, I believe it'll be you. I know of no other place she'd rather be than with her friends in the band, and I know she trusts you more than any other adult in her life right now. I'm not asking you to violate her confidence by telling me where she is. If you don't mind calling me when she contacts you, tell her I'm sorry for what I have done. I really do love her. I just was wrong in the way I tried to show it."

She and I did talk and I passed along her dad's message. She was with a friend and her family and planned to return home in a day or so and I told her how much I appreciated her confidence and trust. Apparently, the only place she felt she truly was important was with her band friends and her band director. She just wanted to be part of something really good in her life...something that gave her a true sense of belonging and worth.

<u>Reminder</u>

During the days and years she was a student of mine, I was focused primarily on the development of her musical and artistic skills while helping guide her through some of the difficult choices of her teenage years. During those same years, she was "teaching me" the lesson of belonging...a lesson so profound she was willing to take great risks to have. I still try to remember that lesson each time I step on the podium. Sometimes, our classrooms might be one of the few places our students feel they truly belong.

"There is no house like the house of belonging."
*David Whyte - **What to Remember When Waking: The Disciplines of an Everyday Life***

<u>Lesson Take-Away:</u> Our classroom, whatever design it may take, might be one of the few places students feel they belong, where they are safe, where they are valued. Never take such opportunities for granted.

Chapter Two:
The Lesson of Loss

The 8th Grade Saxophone Player

"It's so much darker when a light goes out than it would have been if it had never shone."
*— John Steinbeck, **The Winter of Our Discontent***

My first teaching position was a part-time job while I was in college. It was in a very small community in a rural part of the state. The school housed grades one through twelve with only one section of for each grade and a total student population somewhere in the range of three hundred. My band room was a small building...a Quonset hut purchased by the school from an Army Surplus Store...which served as the rehearsal room, my office (a desk and chair), the music library (two filing cabinets), and storage space for all our instruments (shelves on the back wall and one side wall).

I began my part-time work at the school late in the fall of my senior year in college while I was completing the requirements of my undergraduate degree in Music Education. The band met only two days a week for an hour each time but was expected to march in the local Christmas parade, have a Christmas concert, and have a concert at the end of the school year. The first major event I faced when I arrived was the parade. It was not going to be a memorable event.

Small bands in rural settings are very different from larger city bands. This one had approximately 20 students, grades five through twelve, none of whom played tuba and only two of whom played percussion (drums). The ability level of the ensemble was somewhere in the range of a second-year band and the music they performed reflected that level. On second thought, that first parade was, in fact, quite memorable...one bass drummer, one snare drummer, no tubas, and a collection of various instruments being played by young students as they marched, actually they walked, down the main street of the little town. The parents loved it, but I suspect the community members wondered if the students had a teacher or if they were self-taught. As I said, quite memorable. One not easily forgotten.

Our concert rehearsals were spent working on the basics of learning to play the instruments and a little "real music" (sheet music) each day. Small bands are different. They truly do rely on fellow ensemble members for success. That phrase was used regularly in rehearsals, but with a band the size and instrumentation I had, it REALLY was true.

That fact was made uncomfortably clear to me one day when I showed up for class and our senior trumpet player (we had only three in the section: the senior and two intermediate level players) was absent. When I inquired as to his absence, the students explained the reason he was not in school that day was because he was home sleeping. Their cows had gotten out of their pens the night before and he and his family had been up all night getting the cows back. Small bands in rural settings are very different. Everyone knows everyone else...and pretty much everything about everyone else.

It was in this setting I found Mary, my 8th grade alto saxophone player, and her older sister who played flute. They were delightful students, as were all the others, and seemed very appreciative they had someone who would teach them. In fact, the two of them gave me a conductor's baton as a Christmas present, even though I had been their teacher for only a few weeks. It was just a conductor's baton, one that did not even have a case or container. Just a baton. One wrapped in tissue paper and tied with a simple bow. But it was very special to me because it was a gesture of sincere appreciation and gratitude from two students in my first band, a gift I would hold dear for many years.

Later in the spring Mary was often absent. The students just said she was sick. Later, they said she was very sick and was in the hospital. Her sister said she had something wrong with her blood but they hoped she could get better. She didn't. One spring afternoon, when I arrived at the school, the principal met me to tell me Mary had passed away the night before. She had struggled with Leukemia for many months and finally lost the battle. I didn't know how to react or how to proceed. I just knew I wanted to be with my band students in this time of sorrow.

I was waiting in our little room when the students arrived for rehearsal. Back then, especially in small rural schools, there were no school-wide counseling services or grief counselors on site for students in times of crisis. Students and teachers addressed tragedies as best they could by depending on each other to comfort and support one another. For the most part, teachers were left to their own strategies and procedures, and wisdom, for helping students in times of grief.

The members of my little band were unusually quiet as they unpacked their instruments, moved to their seats, and waited for me to speak to them. Here I was, this twenty-one-year-old college student who was still working through his personal and professional philosophies of life and work. But my students were looking to me for help in dealing with the death of their friend, a friend who only a few weeks before had been with them in rehearsals, a person they saw every day in school and in their community, a member of their special little band.

I was struggling to find my way in this time of crisis, so I said to my little band, "Today's a sad day for all of us. I haven't known Mary as long as you have, but she always made me feel I was important to her. Rather than playing our instruments today, maybe it would be a good time for us to talk about her and remember her and what she meant to each of us. So, instead of rehearsing our music, let's talk about Mary. I'm going to give anyone who wishes to speak the opportunity to say something about her and what she meant to them."

No one said anything for a while as they sat silently and gathered their thoughts, then our senior trumpet player and retriever of wandering cows, raised his hand. I recognized him and he said, "Mary always made me feel special, even when I didn't think I was. I'll always remember that about her." After a while another student spoke, "Mary always would smile when she saw me. Nobody else did that." Another, "Mary may not have been the best player in our band, but she told me that being in band and playing music was one of the best parts of her life." Yet another, "Mary always made me feel I was one of her best friends and always made me feel good when I was around her." Next, "I didn't know Mary was so sick. She never seemed that way. She was always kind to others, especially me, and I'm glad we got to play in the band together. Music will always make me think about her." And lastly, after what seemed a long period of silence, one young man finally found the courage, and his words, and he said, "Mary was my friend, and I'll always miss her. But when I play in the band, and we make music together, that'll always remind me of her. And that won't ever go away."

Such simple and profound statements of loss and grieving from those too young to understand the difficulties and complexities of life.

I closed our class time by telling my students they would always be very special to me because they were my "first band." I thanked them for helping me to deal with the loss of one of my students, their friend and classmate. Because of them and the beautiful tributes they had spoken about Mary, I would be a better teacher...and a better person. Sometimes, simplicity in dealing with tragic events in our lives brings peace in ways not expected. They taught me, their band director, a lesson in dealing with loss.

<u>Reminder</u>

On a shelf in my home office lies a conductor's baton. Just a baton. It's not in a case and it's too long for practical use in rehearsal. But it always will be one of my most special gifts because it came from an 8th-grade saxophone player and her sister as an expression of gratitude for what I meant in their lives. That gift, just a baton, and the beautiful memories I have of Mary and how she changed the lives of so many others during her short life, including mine, will always be a reminder of that **Lesson in Loss.**

May love be what you remember most."
— Darcie Sims

<u>Lesson Take-Away:</u> Loss is part of life. For our students, no matter their age, we can be one of the few people, if not the only person, from whom they gather comfort and solace. We should be sensitive to those opportunities that come our way for us to help others. Helping others makes us stronger.

Chapter Three:
The Lesson of Silence (Heard and Unheard)

My 2nd-1st-2nd-1st Chair Clarinet Player

"He who does not understand your silence will probably not understand your words."
— Elbert Hubbard

Depending on the time of the year, or possibly which week of the month it was, she was either my first chair clarinet player or my second chair player. The challenge system we had in place for our high school band program allowed chair challenges only so often and under specific guidelines so as not to have a constant stream of students wishing to re-challenge immediately after losing their chair position. The process was reasonably structured and was not to be taken lightly. However there was this one student who simply was determined to hold the first chair position for our ensemble. And she did...and she didn't...and she did. Such was the process.

What transpired and eventually took place was that she and the person she regularly challenged, or re-challenged, kept the first chair position more or less a temporary and rotating assignment due to their persistence. Less obvious to other band members was that both players increased their technical and musical skills through the pressure they were placing on each other. And our band got better because of the two of them...one of whom hardly spoke, except when addressed, and the other was a social butterfly who never met a stranger. The quiet one was the one whose lesson I almost missed.

I don't think I ever noticed her not paying attention to my instructions from the podium or talking during rehearsal unless she was called on, and when she was, she always responded with correct and insightful answers. For the most part of our time together I thought she simply enjoyed being in the band and playing her clarinet...and winning, and holding, the first chair clarinet position. Only much later did I realize and fully appreciate the significance of the **Lesson of Silence** she was teaching me.

"My 2nd-1st-2nd-1st Chair Clarinet Player," unbeknownst to me, had a great interest in reading and writing poetry and short essays. It was quite by accident some of her writings came to my attention. In fact, had she not left her books and clarinet in my office briefly one afternoon at the end of the school day while she ran an errand, I very likely would not have seen some of her exceptional prose.

Lying on her abandoned clarinet case were several pages of short poems she had written. On top of that collection of scattered pages in clear view of anyone who glanced at it was a handwritten essay entitled something along the line of, "Being Me Until I Can Decide on Something Else." Obviously, I was intrigued by and very interested in her writing, so I simply had to ask her about it when she and her friend returned from their academic mission.

She told me she loved writing and said she tried to write often. I asked her what her favorite subjects were, and she replied that her everyday life gave her many subjects and people about which she could write. With a certain degree of hesitancy, she said she had written about some of her experiences in band and about some of the things I had done and said. I was reluctant to ask to read her writings about me, but I did inquire as to some of her poetry and prose and asked if she would share with me what she felt were her better works, especially the ones she would like for me to read. I was not prepared for what she let me read.

Her observations of her peers and her surroundings were exceptionally keen and highly detailed. The way she treated her sentences and the flow of her words were unusually similar to a beautiful musical phrase...just the right amount of stress and relaxation, the correct proportion of accelerando and rallentando, and the proper blending of consonance and dissonance. Her love of the written and spoken word was obvious through her work. And at such a young age...

I told her how much I enjoyed her ability to write so beautifully and I would certainly enjoy reading more if she would permit. As a result of my continued encouragements and suggestions, she said she had some special collections she would be willing to share with me, but seemed a bit hesitant to tell me what they were about. Finally convinced I truly was interested in reading what she had to offer, she agreed to bring me those special pages. The delightful writings she brought explained her silence...a silence I thought to be an indicator of her shyness or her lack of interest in what was taking place around her. Not the first, nor the last, time I was or would be wrong.

"My 2nd-1st-2nd-1st Chair Clarinet Player" had compiled a list, a booklet if you will, of things, both humorous and unusual, I had said during rehearsals and she was keeping them for future entertainment and consideration. I was certain I hadn't said all the things she had listed, but she assured me she listened to everything I said in rehearsals and made note of the "good ones" as soon as class was over. Sometimes the quotes were too good to wait until rehearsal was finished, so she pretended to be marking her music for a more efficient rehearsal but was in fact jotting down yet another quote she fondly labeled a "Gregory-ism." She wasn't simply being silent; she was listening and collecting.

"My silent 2nd-1st-2nd-1st Chair Clarinet Player" had gathered quotes from the podium and seemed to be concerned I might be upset with her actions...that I might think she was taking things lightly I said, or was laughing at some of my instructions. Nothing was further from the truth. In fact, her quotes brought me a special pleasure; they helped me better understand some of the ways my students possibly received my instructions.

My silent clarinet player jotted down my comment when I said, "We've got to work harder to be better. Right now we're just stuck in the quagmire of mediocracy!" Or one of the many times I said, "It's not how loudly you play; it's how loudly you're heard." Another: "Balancing our ensemble is, in its simplest form, adjusting how loudly sections and passages are heard." Also, "You not only have a responsibility to do well personally; you have that same responsibility to do your best for every other person in our band." And..."Playing in tune is a process, not an event." Lastly, her favorite, "Sometimes you can be better than you think you can."

She gave me copies of those quotes and I assured her I would keep them and treasure them throughout my teaching career, even longer. That seemed to bring her great happiness...as it did me. Such a wonderful teacher for me as she guided me through her **Lesson of Silence**.

<u>Reminder</u>

Many years later "My 2nd-1st-2nd-1st Chair Clarinet Player," now a brilliant and wonderfully successful middle school science teacher, sent me a picture of the announcement board in her classroom on the first day of a new academic year. Displayed in bold print and framed in quotation marks was one quote: "I will never apologize for insisting on excellence."...Dr. David Gregory.

Her silence was not a lack of interest or understanding; it was the polar opposite. My exceptionally gifted clarinet player listened carefully and completely, and silently. The only way something that rare and insightful could happen was if she understood the power of silence.

May we always be aware of and listen to our silent students. They have much to say. The silence of My 2nd-1st-2nd-1st Chair Clarinet Player spoke clearly. Fortunately I was able to hear it.

"The deepest rivers make the least noise."
— Richard Hooker

The Drummer Who Became a Director

"Don't let the noise of others' opinions drown out your own inner voice.
— Steve Jobs

This student was an outgoing, friendly, enthusiastic, and engaging band member. One seemingly everyone liked. He brought positive energy and excitement wherever he went, especially to band rehearsals and performances. He came to my school because of the re-zoning of school districts; I was luckier than I knew. But in the years following, I would realize just how fortunate I was as I watched this young man/talented musician grow into a remarkable teacher and leader of others and make a profound impact on our profession. I never thought he would realize his calling as a teacher/band director and would allow me to share that special career. His silence regarding his love affair with music was not heard.

This particular student, whom I dubbed "The Drummer Who Became a Director," excelled in his music work, but I thought that simply was a precursor to his future calling as a businessman, theologian, medical specialist, or some other highly trained professional. He was my percussion section leader, a remarkable snare drummer/timpanist, and a person who possessed innate qualities of leadership and motivation. I certainly enjoyed having him in my ensembles and believed he enjoyed being part of them. We experienced considerable success with our marching and concert work during his years in my program and he always celebrated the achievements of his fellow band members. He truly was a person who would make an impact on the lives of others. And he did...

I never saw any indication during his first three years with me that "The Drummer Who Became a Director" would become an amazing band director; I assumed he was destined for some other wonderfully successful career. It was sometime midway through his senior year when he came to me to ask where I attended college for my training to become a band director. When I told him, he asked for more information about how to apply for admission, what kind of things would be needed, what musical requirements there were for auditioning, and any other things he might need to know. Even then I was not quick enough to pick up on exactly what he was seeking.

Eventually I asked him why he was asking those things, and he told me he wanted to become a band director.

I was surprised, pleasantly so, that he would consider this special profession as a career pursuit and I asked why he would want to be a band director. His response: "I want to have a band like ours, and I want to make students feel as special and important as you do with us. The amazing things we do together we couldn't do by ourselves." Little did I know, or had I even given thought to the possibility, that the things we did during our daily interactions and our ensemble undertakings would have such an impact on a young person in my class. An impact so significant he would be willing to accept the challenges of traveling many miles from home to study at a university where he knew no one, undertaking training in a profession with which he had only limited exposure, taking "the path less traveled" as a career choice when no one else in his family had chosen this profession, or staying the course through his years of undergraduate studies where he faced financial, social, and peer pressures to choose other options.

I had never considered that he was thinking about teaching music as a career. He never said anything along that line nor did he ever indicate he was interested in becoming a teacher. His silence was unheard...but not wasted.

His undergraduate university years saw him develop further as a wonderful musician/artist and as a person well-grounded in his beliefs and in his abilities to help others become better. There were a number of job offers after graduation, and he chose to begin his successful career as a middle school band director. Over the years, he held several teaching positions, both at the middle school and high school levels, and served as percussion instructor for several colleges. During his more than four decades of service to young people through his guidance and instruction, "The Drummer Who Became a Director" changed the lives of thousands. The silence not heard during his high school years became a voice that helped change his profession. Many times, silence can speak loudly, even when first not heard.

"The Drummer Who Became a Director" continued to impact my life and work throughout our years of working and performing together. He was my student, my peer, a colleague, my friend, and someone whose life and actions helped me become a better teacher and better person— once I heard his silence. What a gift this **Lesson of Silence,** even though I did not hear it at the time, and how beautifully this lesson was taught.

Nothing strengthens authority so much as silence."
— Leonardo da Vinci

<u>Lesson Take-Away:</u> Teachers must always listen for the silence of our students, whatever shape or form it might be found or even when it is disguised in noise. Sometimes the voices of silence call to us more loudly than the noise that surrounds us.

Chapter Four:
The Lesson of Discovery

My Senior Marching Band Student

"The real voyage of discovery consists not in seeking new landscapes, but in having new eyes."
— Marcel Proust

She was a junior in high school and I was her fifth band director in five years. Needless to say, her experiences in band had not provided her with evidence that band director appointments were something that lasted very long. When I came to her school as the newly appointed Director of Bands, she thought of me as "just another teacher," an attitude she expressed to me the following year when she showed up at the beginning of school her senior year and found me once again in the same office as the previous year. Her question to me at that time was, "Why are you back again this year? I thought we'd have a new director."

"My Senior Marching Band Student" was an exceptionally bright and perceptive young person, one who easily understood new concepts and ideas, and one willing to experiment with different approaches to problem-solving and implementing new solutions. In short, she was a great band student...but she was only an average bass clarinet player. Regardless of her less-than-conservatory-level performance abilities, she thoroughly enjoyed being part of the ensemble and her contributions were significant.

My appointment as Director of Bands at this school was my first high school band director position. It came during the summer months, which did not allow a great deal of time to prepare for the transition from teaching junior high to high school, so major changes such as scheduling, personnel, and overall program design for that upcoming fall were not made. However, I did choose not to use bass clarinets in our marching band at that time, primarily because of the awkwardness of marching with the instrument. I asked those students, one of whom was "My Senior Marching Band Student," to march with Bb clarinets. They readily agreed and seemed to enjoy all aspects of the marching season, relieved they did not have to struggle with a bass clarinet on the practice and performance fields. My first year at that school as Director of Bands (and her with her fifth director in as many years) went well. The stage was set for a remarkable discovery by her the next fall.

High school seniors always behave a bit differently than underclass students and "My Senior Marching Band Student" was no exception...possibly because she was more comfortable with me as her only band director to return for a second year with her, or maybe she was just enjoying the "senior-itis" many students display during their final year in high school. Whatever the circumstances, she became more visible around the band room during her spare time and seemed to enjoy spending time with other band students in that environment.

She dropped by my office often to share an opinion, share her position on certain social issues, or to question me as to why I would choose to be a teacher since they were overworked and underpaid. In short, she was an intelligent, engaging, and delightful student who seemed destined for a successful and significant career. And in the following years she did accomplish exactly that, which in hindsight made her **Lesson of Discovery** during her senior year even more meaningful to me.

Mind you we were in the second week of October, dead center of the marching band season and working toward our final events of the year, when "My Senior Marching Band Student," stopped by my office one afternoon after practice. She was as excited as I had ever seen her and she wanted to share that excitement with me. Again, it was **the second week of October**...

Her excitement was so great she didn't even bother to sit as she talked. It seemed that she had made a huge discovery regarding marching band that afternoon and that epiphany was the source of her joy. She said to me, "Mr. Gregory, today during practice, I realized something and it changed everything about being in marching band. You know when we are moving from position to position while playing...I figured out that my foot was supposed to hit the ground on every beat! Every beat my foot hits the ground! Every. Beat! Now it all makes sense!" She was ecstatic, and I was stunned.

It was the second week of October! What had she been doing for the first half of the season while she marched? No! What had she been doing on the field during rehearsals and performances for three and a half years? After a brief pause for my disbelief to settle, I inquired further into her enlightenment. I didn't go too far with my questions for fear of lessening the thrill of her discovery, but I was more than a bit intrigued with what had transpired. She offered no detailed explanation other than while she was "marching" that afternoon, she "just realized" everyone's feet were hitting the ground on the beat. And suddenly, it all made sense.

This was a first for me, and it caused me to examine my teaching methods when instructing marching band techniques. What had I not done, or what had I not made clear for understanding? I simply could not come up with a satisfactory answer, especially since "My Senior Marching Band Student" was unusually bright and perceptive. But then I remembered a quote I heard somewhere along the way years before..."Not all popcorn kernels pop at the same time." Not a very good explanation, and certainly not much of an academic approach, but somehow this bright and capable student figured out the physical relationship between movement and music, but only after several years of participation. Thankfully she did, and we still had four more marching band performances for her to demonstrate her newly found kinesthetic talents.

I shared her excitement even though I was somewhat chagrined. I had not been observant enough to discover her apparent phasing/out-of-step participation for a year and a half. But after I thought about it a while, I realized our students understand at different times, and under different circumstances, the concepts we strive to impart and the skills we attempt to teach. Her "discovery" was no less important and exciting to her than that of a beginning band student (or any other student of ours) when a new concept is captured or a new skill is mastered.

May we as teachers never lose the ability to recognize and appreciate the **"Lesson of Discovery"** of our students. Those discoveries can bring great excitement and reward to them. May we as teachers always be open and receptive to discoveries in our own lives...ones our students give us while they are "teaching" us.

<u>Reminder</u>

As expected, "My Senior Marching Band Student," through hard work, dedication, and perseverance (remember, it took only three and a half years to figure out the marching band thing), became a successful lawyer and helped many who otherwise could have suffered loss. She eventually held positions at some of the highest levels of our judiciary system, but never lost the search for and thrill of new discoveries in her life. Thank you, "My Senior Marching Band Student," for sharing your **Lesson of Discovery** with your band director. You challenged me many years ago, without knowing it, and inspired me in future years in my search for discoveries in my life.

> *"Every block of stone has a statue inside it and it is the task of the sculptor to find it."*
> *— Michelangelo*

<u>Lesson Take-Away:</u> Discovery is new and fresh no matter the age of the discoverer. Discovery brings with it the possibility for enlightenment and excitement. Teachers are given the privilege of helping guide students toward new aspects of their lives...no matter the age of the student. Discovery is always new.

Chapter Five:
The Lesson of Perseverance

My Beginning Flute Player

"You may encounter many defeats, but you must not be defeated."
— Maya Angelou

Every beginning band student is a wonderful mixture of challenges and potential and it is up to the teacher to address them with insight and acumen. Simply by being part of the band class, each student brings to the teacher yet another riddle of, "I hope you can figure me out and teach me to play my instrument." Such was the case with "My Beginning Flute Player," and never before had I faced a challenge that taught **me** so much.

She wanted to play the flute because it had always been her favorite instrument in the band, and because her older sister had done so several years earlier. Quite simply, she could not wait until she had the opportunity to start band classes and begin learning to play the flute. Without a doubt she was the most enthusiastic of all the beginners in my class that year. That enthusiasm never waned and her efforts never lessened...both of which helped me to understand the **Lesson of Perseverance.**

In teaching my beginner band classes, once the students understood the basics of instrument care, playing positions, tone production, posture, and counting rhythms, I required each of them to turn in practice records every week which were signed by a parent/guardian. The amount of practice time required depended on the progress level of the class, but it was usually a minimum of fifteen minutes each day rather than a total for the week. Without fail, "My Beginning Flute Player" turned in her weekly practice records, each with more than the required time. The only problem was she could not produce a tone on her flute. Nothing but air.

I worked with her using every technique I knew. I had other flute teachers and players work with her, but with the same non-results. We were discouraged, but "My Beginning Flute Player" never showed the slightest hint of frustration. She seemed content with her huffing and puffing and "poo-ing" and "thu-ing" as she moved her fingers for different pitches. I figured somewhere along the way her sound would show up, so we continued...she worked diligently (and happily) and I continued to experiment with ways to help her produce a tone. Nothing but air...

The practice routines of "My Beginning Flute Player" continued throughout the year, each week's sheet showing hours of weekly practice, but there was never a flute tone to show for her efforts, just air being blown across the tone hole. She never failed to turn in a practice sheet, nor did her dedication ever lessen. And during it all (class time and private practice time), did she ever seem discouraged with her efforts.

I did the best I could to work with her, but in the very limited time I met with the beginning band class I had only a few minutes to work with her individually. I simply could not solve this problem, so I decided to let her enjoy her time in band class, hoping that over the summer or when she reached middle school the following year her teacher would have better luck finding ways to meet this challenge.

Fast forward. The middle school she attended was not where I taught so I lost contact with her for several years and did not see her again until her junior year of high school when I dropped by that school for a special band rehearsal. After so many years I did not recognize her at first when I saw her before rehearsal, but there was an even greater surprise waiting for me once it started.

We visited a bit before rehearsal and, quite honestly, I was surprised she was still in the band after such a struggle in beginning band. I thought, maybe she just enjoyed the social aspect of being with her friends in that environment, as she was a shy person, and band participation gave her a "school family." Imagine my shock when rehearsal began and I saw her take her place as first chair flute/piccolo player in the ensemble. I was amazed!

How could this student who for an entire year in beginning band could not produce a single tone on her flute now be the first chair flute player in a very fine high school band? Maybe it was because her other middle school teacher figured out how to solve the riddle, or maybe somewhere along the line things just "clicked"...or maybe she <u>simply refused to give up</u> on something she wanted so badly and eventually figured out how to produce a tone. Whatever the case, "My Beginning

Flute Player" had beaten the odds in several categories and was now the principal flutist in her high school band.

Once I had recovered from my wonderful surprise, I began to think of the effort and determination it must have taken for a fifth-grade student to persevere in the face of so many seemingly insurmountable odds. As I sat there in that rehearsal listening to her play so beautifully as she led her section, I could not help but let her lesson of "staying the course" and "never losing sight of what could be" instruct me as how I must never underestimate the value and power of perseverance.

<u>Reminder</u>

Years later as I think back on that wonderful student, I have no doubt this young lady experienced much success in her life...simply because she was not willing to give up on something important to her. Her beautiful story of success helped me "keep on keeping on" many times during my career. Thank you, "My Beginning Flute Player," for reminding me of that important lesson...a lesson that impacted a generation of students.

My Drummer Who Almost Wasn't

"Courage doesn't always roar. Sometimes courage is the quiet voice
at the end of the day saying, 'I will try again tomorrow.'"
— *Mary Anne Radmacher*

Band instruction usually began in the fifth grade, sixth at the latest, in the school system where I taught. Occasionally there would be a situation when a student moved into our district and had not had the opportunity to participate in band classes before the sixth grade but wished to do so. When those occasions arose, respective teachers would do their best to accommodate the beginner in hopes of being able to integrate that student into regular classroom activities as soon as possible and practical. I had experienced a handful of such beginning student situations at this level, but never with high school band.

"My Drummer Who Almost Wasn't" approached me one day early in his Freshman year in high school to ask if he could join the band. This engaging young man with a world-class smile and a personality that invited others to be his friend said he had not been in the band at his previous school, but had seen ours and wondered if he could join. When I asked what instrument he played, he responded "none," but said he was willing, and wanted, to learn to play the snare drum. He wanted to be part of our marching band. From that first meeting, I was a fan of this young man. It was hard not to like him and something about him said, "Give me a chance. You won't be disappointed." He was right.

I explained that our marching band was, for the most part, a compilation of our entire band program and that he would need to register for and be a member of one of our band classes and would need to be prepared to work more than just during class time in order to catch up with the ability levels of the other ensemble members. I said I would meet with him and try to bring him up to speed on some of the basics of music notation, reading music, counting and playing rhythms, and performing in an ensemble. He was unusually receptive to my suggestions and seemed eager to undertake this series of new challenges.

"My Drummer Who Almost Wasn't" made excellent progress and he spent a great deal of time in the band room outside rehearsal hours. He was tireless in his individual practicing and his enthusiasm only grew stronger with each new skill level he achieved. I think his excitement over his accomplishments reached a high point when he came into my office one day to ask if he could "check out" a marching snare drum to take home in order to practice for becoming a member of the marching band. Who could turn down such a request, and who would not try to find a place in the marching band for a student so eager to be part of it?

Once he earned a position in the percussion section, his enthusiasm increased exponentially. He was one of the first to be in position on the field for practice; he stayed a bit longer after we finished in order to put up his drums properly (after he had cleaned them); he took every opportunity to ask questions of his section leader, and others, as to how to become a better player; he was a model for all the other band members to follow. Apparently, this young man had found something in his life that brought unusual excitement and reward, and I was thrilled for him.

Throughout his high school years, not only did "My Drummer Who Almost Wasn't" march in the percussion section of our marching band, he also learned to play the tuba, and eventually earned a position in the tuba section of our concert band. Never did his enthusiasm wane for marching band participation, nor apparently did his enjoyment of performing as a tuba player in one of our concert ensembles.

This young man had found something that seemingly changed his life for the better. I was pleased he was such a terrific band member and enjoyed his time with us so much. He seemed to bring inspiration to others wherever he went. He was the kind of student all teachers would treasure to have as part of their legacy.

Years later, I discovered that he had learned his snare drum rudiments by practicing on a broken coffee table in his home and had, in his own words, "learned brass fingering first…using an old trumpet a mailman kindly gave me." Very seldom had I been so fortunate as to have a student of such vision and dedication and commitment. There are few others who could have, and would have, accomplished all he did. It is no wonder this very special person achieved greatness in his personal and professional life.

Decades passed before I was made aware of the extent of his dedication to his commitment during those years as well as to the impact his life and work would have on countless others. A number of years following his high school graduation, "My Drummer Who Almost Wasn't" sent me a message via social media. His note started off with, "Hi, Dr.

Gregory. You probably don't remember me, but I'm the drummer you allowed to start in beginning band in high school. I just wanted to reach out to you and say 'Thank You' and let you know some of how my life turned out after being in your band" *(personal thought: anytime a student starts a message with, "You probably don't remember me," I believe the student is saying "I sure hope you remember me.")*.

He proceeded to tell me that after high school he attended college and was in the marching band as a snare drummer (lead snare for most of the time), also played the tuba—sometimes the euphonium—and enjoyed four years of university band activities. He then entered graduate school, where he studied Computer Science and Math, served in the Armed Forces and eventually retired as a Lieutenant Colonel in the United States Army, worked in financial planning for several years, and eventually retired from a wonderfully successful career as an engineer with a global marketing institution.

He provided additional information as to how he had been given opportunities to help others...possibly the way he had been helped. Again, in his own words: "After work, I tutored trigonometry and pre-calculus to inner-city kids, and everywhere I moved there were students who needed help with algebra, geometry, and pre-calculus. If they made it past that, they were usually headed in the right direction. I also tutored computer science to engineering students. One lesson music taught me is that 'not understanding' is often just a matter of lacking resources and exposure. So I've always tried to meet students where they are."

And remember, this is the student who learned his snare drum rudiments "on a broken coffee table" and "learned brass fingerings...using an old trumpet a mailman kindly gave me." Is it any wonder this remarkable person changed the lives of thousands?

"My Drummer Who Almost Wasn't" finished his message to me by saying his time in our band gave him the confidence to explore new possibilities and to try things he once might have thought were unattainable. His final comments to me were those of thanks for giving him a chance to prove to himself he could accomplish much in life if he simply kept trying, even when others might not have thought it possible. All he needed was the opportunity.

Sometimes I wonder what might have happened if I had not made an exception and allowed him to begin his work in band at such a late stage. Yet another lesson taught and a lesson learned. Thank you, "My Drummer Who Almost Wasn't." You made me a better teacher and helped make my life richer. I am fortunate you shared your "lesson" with me. Your story inspires me...

<u>Reminder</u>

The Lesson of Perseverance reminded me many times how small actions, even something as simple as allowing a student to participate in the ensemble in a non-traditional format, can open pathways to future success. Or maybe an act as uncomplicated as a beginning band student working so hard to accomplish something that seemed unlikely can remind us never to underestimate the power of the desire of someone wanting to do and become something exceptional. We must remind ourselves not to give up, even when they "can't seem to make a sound on their flute." Our students need to see that in us.

Lesson Take Away: It is said many times that the hardest part of getting started is getting started. If true, as teachers we must realize the second hardest part is continuing forward. Students, and teachers, become discouraged, but we must find ways to persevere, both personally and professionally. Our students see that quality in us, and they can also recognize the lack of that same quality.

Chapter Six:
The Lesson of Humor

Being Late

"I always arrive late at the office, but I make up for it by leaving early."
— Charles Lamb

One of the "worn, weary, and over-used" sayings in the band world is, "Early is on time and on time is late." Of course, this simple statement is in itself a bit counterintuitive through the way the phrases are set in conflict with one another. However, band students completely understand the meaning no matter how the words are placed: be at rehearsal well before it is scheduled to begin.

So many of us directors preach this message to our students, and we attempt to model the expected behavior by starting rehearsals exactly when scheduled and not allowing non-essentials to delay those beginnings. If our students are trained in this behavior, they will act accordingly with very few exceptions. It becomes part of their personal and professional habits. In fact, my students were so indoctrinated with this philosophy that at times I had parents come to me asking for their child not to be penalized for being late to a rehearsal. It was their fault, not the child's. The parent took full responsibility for the transgression and promised to try to do better in the future. One parent even brought a note to me regarding **his** actions, not his child's, which caused the tardiness. Perhaps I overshot the target with this bit of training. But at least the students relayed to their parents the significance of rehearsal times. There was clarity on that point.

Nevertheless, the tardiness rule is a necessity for all ensembles that aspire to excellence, and it must be ingrained in the students as they share the common goals of achievement. I was fortunate to have a supportive community for my high school band and the tardiness issue was never a significant problem. Only many years later did I realize just how deeply this sense of being on time was ingrained in my students.

At a reunion of my high school band, possibly the twenty-fifth year of my starting my work at that school, one of my former trumpet players came to me for some catching up on the last quarter of a century of our lives. During that chat he recounted some of the great memories he had of our time together and some of the achievements of our band while he was a member. Good times for certain.

While we were visiting, he mentioned the emphasis on punctuality in our rehearsals and how that was such an important part of his high school training. He said he lived in constant fear he would be late and have to walk into rehearsal after it had begun and have all his peers stare at him because of his apparent human weaknesses and lack of self-discipline. Horror upon horror if I had to stop the rehearsal for a late comer to wander in... something no one in the band wished to experience personally.

We laughed about this and other parts of our times together and he mentioned, somewhat casually, but not totally convincingly, that even after all these years, he still experienced mild to moderate panic when he was late to work. He just couldn't shake that feeling of guilt for showing up late when others had already arrived and were being productive. And after a brief pause, he said..."And I own the company! I'm the President and CEO but when I show up late, I still feel I need to bring a note explaining my reason for being tardy. Twenty-five years later!" Again, maybe I overshot the target a bit...

The Theory Class

"Education is learning what you didn't even know you didn't know."
— Daniel J. Boorstin

My Theory Class was, next to my Symphonic Band rehearsal, the highlight of my teaching day. Highly motivated students, several of whom were planning on being music majors in college, all with the desire to know more about the structure and function of the elements of music. I tried to encompass as much music history as appropriate into the instruction since many of the analyses and applications of harmonic design came from and were directly tied into the historical eras of musical composition. It was a great class.

One day when I was attempting to engage the class with the beauty and functionality of the Dominant 7th chord, somehow, I completely lost control of the direction of the class. We were discussing that delightful harmonic device and I was laboring to explain and demonstrate how such chords were used and how they resolved when leading to another chord.

The students were taking notes and some were asking questions...good ones, so I was thinking I was doing a great job of helping these young scholars add to their musical vocabularies. They were even to the point they could identify the Dominant 7th quite easily during the ear training part of our work. Things seemed to be going well, and I was about to embark on an introductory discussion of the even more exotic Secondary Dominant 7th chord when it happened. The rope began to unravel.

I was demonstrating on our marker board the V7 chord resolutions as I was preparing the class for the role of the Secondary Dominant. Assuming the students were following along with enthusiasm appropriate to their age and academic levels, I turned to the class to inquire if there were questions or observations. One student raised his hand and said, "Mr. Gregory, do you know one of your sideburns is longer than the other?"

Momentarily, I thought I was having a problem with my hearing and had misunderstood his "question." Not so. I mumbled weakly, "What?" He repeated his question, and I found myself completely flummoxed as I stood before this group of terrific students. I was speechless and didn't have a clue as to how I should respond...or even if I should respond.

When I found my words, I responded with something along the line of, "What are you talking about? They're the same length." That comment was met with a resounding class response, "Oh no they're not! Your right one is longer than your left." I stood motionless, hands to the sides of my face, checking the length of each sideburn, in what moments before had been an environment of musical and academic pursuit but suddenly had collapsed into a full-blown discussion of the inaccuracies of my morning shaving routine. How could something like this happen?

I fell into the trap further by asking yet another question: "Why would you ever notice anything so insignificant as that...even if it were true?" Their answer: "We notice <u>everything</u> you do and say. We even know how many pairs of pants you have for work and that you wear only two pairs of shoes for school, plus the pair you have for marching band rehearsals."

We continued that somewhat uncomfortable conversation *(on my part at least; the students were loving it)* with several other "observations" of theirs as they enjoyed telling me of some of my other idiosyncrasies and unusual habits. Surprisingly, they enjoyed laughing at and with me more than discussing and investigating the mysteries of the Dominant 7th chord. Teenagers can be strange and wonderful creatures...

I still wasn't totally convinced my right sideburn was longer than my left, but I double checked them each day for several days following that theory lesson...just to make certain. And I was extra careful with my shaving practices once I was aware my students were noticing. Now, if I could get them to focus as well on their musical tasks...but that wouldn't be nearly so much fun for them. Teenagers...go figure.

<u>Reminder</u>

Needless to say, I left that class a changed person. Never again would I take for granted the degree to which my students followed my actions and spoken words so closely. I was reminded once again of the quote attributed to Ralph Waldo Emerson, "What you do speaks so loudly I cannot hear what you are saying."

<u>Lesson Take-Away:</u> _"Man is the only animal that laughs and weeps; for he is the only animal that is struck with the difference between what things are, and what they ought to be" (William Hazlitt). It is important our students see us laugh at those things worthy of laughter. Laughter does not make us less of a teacher; it makes us more of a human._

Chapter Seven:
The Lesson of Caring and Sharing

The Committee Chair

"Three keys to more abundant living: caring about others, daring for others, sharing with others."
— William Arthur Ward

The university at which I taught was in many ways very much like other such institutions, and in many ways very different from those places. We had the usual distribution of those students whose parents could afford to pay for their college education, those who were borrowing additional money to assist what could be provided by their family, quite a few who were on other forms of financial assistance, and many who were on work-study programs and struggling to pay college costs. Then there were those whose families could provide no money for their education and who had desperately few financial resources on which they could rely. My university did remarkable things to help all our students, but especially those who had very little or virtually no financial resources.

Daily necessities and commonplace purchases seemingly were insurmountable obstacles to those students in the last group, yet somehow, they persisted in spite of their crushingly difficult financial circumstances. We had a significant percentage of our student population who fell into that last category; in that way our university was different from many others. I had several of these students in my ensemble who were pursuing a degree in music, wishing to become teachers. My situation was perfect for the Lesson of Caring and Sharing to be taught to me.

The first concert of the fall semester was only a few days away, and during one of our final rehearsals I was in the process of addressing last minute details of our performance. Things such as arrival time on stage, warm-up format, ensemble protocol during performance, tuning procedure, and concert dress would all soon be standard procedure but had to be reviewed carefully before the first concert of the season.

Dress for this concert was to be "Concert Black," not to be confused with "Concert Formal." I asked ensemble members to wear all black.

Black pants and black shirt. Women could wear a black blouse, with sleeves, and black slacks, or they could wear a black dress; men were to wear a long-sleeved black dress shirt, no tie. No tee shirts for anyone. The rule was: The less skin showing the better. Everyone seemed to understand these guidelines so we moved forward and successfully finished the rehearsal as we prepared for our concert later in the week.

I had returned to my office once rehearsal was finished when one of the freshmen in the ensemble stopped by to say she didn't have a black blouse and the only black pants she had were jeans. She didn't know what she could do and she was embarrassed to tell me she didn't have the clothes needed for performance...and she had no money to buy any. She hadn't mentioned it earlier because, as she said, "I hoped something would work out." (*Yet another reminder to this conductor that hope is not a plan...*)

One of the senior members of the ensemble, our percussion section leader, was standing nearby and overheard the conversation but waited until the freshman left to come into my office to chat. She said she understood what the young lady was going through and, with my permission, she would "take care of the situation." She was confident things would work out but assured me she would let me know if she ran into difficulties; she had experienced a similar situation a few years earlier and knew many of the challenges the freshman was facing. I thanked her for her concern and her willingness to help the younger student. She replied that she had been helped when she was in great need, and that help had given her the chance to continue her studies. She would, as she said, "handle things."

Two days later, the day of our concert, the freshman came into my office wearing a huge and happy smile, excited to tell me she was ready for the concert and that I would be amazed with her new concert wear. I shared her excitement and asked her to tell me more. I was anxious to hear the back story on this remarkable transformation.

She was thrilled, and surprised, to discover there was a "Senior Award," given during the week of the first concert of the fall semester. It was organized by senior band members and awarded to a freshman member who had demonstrated an exemplary work ethic and positive attitude during the first month of the academic year. The award was announced each year just prior to the first concert of the season...**and she had been chosen as the winner this year!**

The "Award" was $100 cash and an invitation to join several other band members who were headed to the local Goodwill Store for some fall shopping as they prepared for the upcoming year. Her excitement and gratitude and the significance of what this meant to her brought her to tears. She simply stopped talking and stood in front of my desk until she could find her words again. When she did, in a voice barely above a whisper, she said, "Dr. Gregory, this money...this award...saved me. Now I have a chance to be part of something I never thought I could. I can't tell you how much this means." Not wanting her to feel embarrassed with her tears, I joined her with some of my own. Always thinking of my students...

Later that afternoon as we were setting the stage for the evening's concert, I spoke to the senior member who had approached me with a plan. Apparently, <u>she</u> was the committee for the "Senior Award" and had, as she said she would, "taken care of the issue." I thanked her for what she and some others had done with their shopping expedition to the Goodwill Store and told her how deeply appreciative the freshman was.

When I finished expressing my gratitude to her and telling her of the profound impact her actions had on the freshman, she stopped what she was doing, stood silently for a few seconds, then looked me in the eye and simply said, "Dr. Gregory, you don't have to tell <u>me</u> how things like that can change a person. I know. I personally know what something like that can do. It can change your life. Mine was. I'm just glad I was there to hear her conversation with you. I think we did well with 'The Award' this year. Don't you? This one felt really good."

<h3 style="text-align:center"><u>Reminder</u></h3>

Lives changed. Lessons learned. The student is the teacher and the teacher becomes the student. Yes, my caring and giving senior band member, chair of the "Senior Award" committee, <u>you</u> did really well with this one. Really, really well, my young scholar. Thank you for the Lesson in Caring and Giving. I never cease to be inspired by the good things people are willing to do for those truly in need. Thank you, Committee Chair. Your caring and your actions humbled me.

"Never believe that a few caring people can't change the world.
Indeed, it is the only thing that ever has."
— Margaret Mead

"Service to others is the rent you pay for your room here on earth."
— Maya Angelou

<u>Lesson Take-Away:</u> Caring is loving; loving is caring. Our students are placed in our care. We teach them caring through <u>our</u> acts of caring for others. We teach them love by showing love for others. Our classrooms, and our lives, are full of opportunities to demonstrate both.

Chapter Eight:
The Lesson of Being Hurt

The Contest

"Winning is a state of mind that embraces everything you do."
— Bryce Courtenay, ***The Power of One***

The National Bicentennial Committee announced in 1975 that a Bicentennial Band Contest featuring bands from the thirteen original colonies would be held in the summer of 1976 as part of the bicentennial celebration of our nation's founding. Those thirteen states were asked to devise a system through which respective winners would be chosen to represent their state in a week-long "Festival of the Colonies" contest in Allentown, Pennsylvania. State winners would be announced in 1975, and preparation for the national competition in the areas of concert performance, half-time performance, parade, and military inspection would begin. It would be a contest unlike any other this generation had experienced. I felt my band at Hardaway High School had an excellent chance of winning this contest as we had received only the highest ratings in our state concert evaluations and our marching band had been equally as successful in contest and festival events.

The state of Georgia, working with the Band Division of the state Music Educators Association, established criteria for choosing our official representative. A panel of three judges was named, and those three highly respected directors listened to and ranked recordings submitted by those bands who wished to be considered for this once-in-a-lifetime honor. That same three-member panel of adjudicators would travel the state in the spring of 1975 and observe a live rehearsal of bands as part of the evaluation process of those who had applied for consideration. During this onsite visit, the panel would also evaluate the ensemble in the area of sightreading, one of the aspects of the yearly state adjudication system for bands in Georgia.

Late in the spring of 1975, a composite sheet of the scores of the concert and sightreading results for all participating bands was sent to the directors so each school would be aware of its ranking in comparison with others. Several schools withdrew from the process at that time, apparently because of their ranking and the fact that mathematically they did not feel there was a realistic chance of winning the contest with only one category remaining...that of field show competition which would be held in the fall of 1975.

My band was ranked first in concert and first in sightreading. Mathematically we would be the winners if we simply showed up for and participated in the fall marching adjudication. The other bands, because of their place in the scoring rubric, faced the very unlikely prospect of winning, unless we dropped out. As I said, all we had to do to win was travel to the competition site and participate. And we did...and we did.

My band placed second in the marching competition that evening, first in the overall rankings, and was named the Official Bicentennial Band for the State of Georgia and would represent our state in the summer of 1976 in the National Bicentennial Band Contest of the thirteen original colonies. Our students were ecstatic, our school was proud, band parents were thrilled, and our community gladly announced we were representing Georgia at the national level. It truly was an honor unlike any other...one which brought wonderful recognition to our students, our band, our school, our parents, and our community.

Many weeks of intense planning and preparation followed the fall marching contest and subsequent announcement of our band as the state winner. Working closely with the State Bicentennial Committee, local school system, city government, and our band parents' organization, sufficient funding was provided for the purchase of needed equipment, new band uniforms, travel expenses, rehearsal assistants, and any other appropriate expenses associated with the national contest. It was a whirlwind of activities during the winter of 1975 and spring of 1976. There was an excitement and work ethic demonstrated by our students never seen before, a "oneness of purpose" if you will...and appropriately so. This was going to be our biggest challenge yet. But, as the saying goes, we were all on the same page with this one...without a doubt.

Fast forward to the week-long contest in Allentown, PA. Upon arrival at the airport, we were greeted by our local host band, Slatington High School, with whose members our students would be housed during our week of competition. Thus began several days of making new friends and sharing music...days that would change all of us, some more than others, for the rest of our lives.

As the week progressed and the various aspects of competition unfolded, the stronger bands became more obvious. There were several other band directors traveling with us and they provided regular updates on how the other bands were doing. Some of the bands had concert performances in the morning while others had field competition that evening. The schedule would be rotated the following day, allowing only one major competitive event per day per band. One day was set aside separately for parade inspection and competition for all the bands.

The weather was spectacular all week. Beautiful spring weather had arrived in the Pocono Mountains and our travelers were enjoying a respite from the hot and humid weather of south Georgia where summer already had arrived. But the beautiful weather left us the afternoon we were scheduled for our evening field competition. There were heavy rains predicted for our area...and those predictions were 100% correct.

The rains were extremely heavy but most bands managed to find a way to perform, only to a partially filled stadium. The general public had left when the rain arrived and for the most part all who remained were in some way connected to the participating bands of the evening. A few of the bands performed when the rain stopped periodically while others of us performed in the rain. Our show was during a downpour, but our students rose to the challenge and presented one of their very best performances ever, solidifying their sense of purpose and confirming their status as a "band family" even more so. Everyone on the field "looked just like everybody else. Nobody could tell us apart."

Two evenings later at the grand finale gathering of all participants, category and overall winners were announced. Our field show presentation was declared to be the most outstanding of the week and we were named National Bicentennial Band Contest Marching Champions. We finished in second place in the concert performance division and second in the overall contest behind the spectacular Fort Hunt High School Band of Virginia. We could not have been happier; we had done our best and, as the saying goes, "left it all on the stage." Our hard work and dedication had paid off and our students had earned national honors for their efforts. Another such honor came as an invitation to perform that fall for an even larger national audience.

The Bus Lists

"A torn jacket is soon mended, but hard words bruise the heart of a child."
— Henry Wadsworth Longfellow

One of the judges for the Bicentennial Band Contest was the Director of Bands at a well-known university, and he was also the entertainment director for the Detroit Lions professional football team. Shortly after the Bicentennial Contest he extended an invitation to us as the Bicentennial Contest Marching Band Champions to perform for a Detroit Lions game in the fall. Once again, our students were thrilled to be recognized for their hard work, this time with the opportunity to perform before an audience of nearly 80,000 spectators.

As time drew near for us to leave Columbus, Georgia and travel to Pontiac, Michigan and perform in the Pontiac Silverdome, we were busily taking care of trip details such as bus lists (students signed up by grades starting with the seniors), rooming lists (same sign-up procedure), equipment details, and the myriad of other small things required for long-distance travel. Not long before our departure date, my principal called me into his office for a meeting. I assumed he wanted to make certain everything was set for our trip. Not so.

I reported to his office and as soon as I was seated, the first thing he asked me was, "How many Black students do you have in the band?" (The process of racially integrating public schools in the South was progressing more slowly than in the North). I was shocked. I had no idea what the demographics of my band were. I had never thought of my students in that light. I responded that I honestly had no idea but that I had a <u>total</u> of 174 members in the band.

My answer was not acceptable. He wanted to know how many Black students had signed up for each bus. Again, I didn't know. Students signed up to be with their friends. He explained to me that he wanted the Black students in the band to be equally distributed among the four buses we would be using. His reasoning: he did not want my band traveling to Detroit, Michigan with all the Black students assigned to one bus and White students on the other three. For the first time, I was forced to consider the young people I taught in a way where the color of their skin was the overriding factor. In stark contradiction to the teachings of Dr. Martin Luther King, Jr., I now had to view my students "by the color of their skin rather than the content of their character."

Later that afternoon at rehearsal I had to make that announcement to my band. The first reaction from all the students was shock. Then disappointment. Then anger. Then hurt and sadness. As I tried to explain the position of our school administration, students began to cry. Male and female alike. Black and White. All tears were the same color. It was as if something had been lost and would not be found again. We had passed through a door and it had closed behind us. Soon I had to stop talking to those young people who were my students because I had not yet learned how to find my words through my own tears.

My dedicated, hard-working, caring, goofy, unique, and wonderful teenagers were being told they were different from one another, they had to view each other differently, the incredible work we had done and the things we had accomplished <u>together</u> now must be viewed through racially divided glasses, and the love and shared and admiration they had for one another somehow was conditional in the eyes of our administration. A hard and hurtful lesson to place on the shoulders of anyone...but especially on those of young adults who simply wanted to do and accomplish great things. These were just ordinary, everyday students who had found ways to do extraordinary things.

After rehearsal one of my flute players who would be reassigned to another bus came into my office, still shedding tears of hurt, and said to me, "Mr. Gregory, this is the first time as a member of our band I've ever been made to feel different from anyone else. Everywhere else in our school the Black/White issue is always a thing, but never in our band. For the first time, our principal has made us feel like we have to be treated differently in band too, that we're not the same." She spoke these beautiful and heartfelt words as tears ran down her face, and standing beside her as she said them was her best friend, who was White...with her own tear-filled eyes.

Many tears were shed; much sadness was shared; a deeper understanding was gained of just how special our band was in the lives of each member; and possibly a lesson for later life was learned. That day, as I watched those young people struggle with something not of their making, was one that helped better shape my philosophy of teaching, and of life. Some wounds never quite heal...nor should they. Some lessons need to remain clear.

The Reunion

"The wound is the place where the Light enters you."
— Rumi

Some forty-five years later at a reunion of band members during the decade I was at that school, I once again saw former students, some of whom I had not seen in nearly fifty years. The organizers of the event decided the title of the gathering should be **"One More Time."** No idea where that came from.

As the students, many of whom were now grandparents, were arriving, I was doing my best to meet and greet them individually. A small group arrived together, four close friends from those years of the Bicentennial Contest, three Black and one White. As they approached me, each embraced me and held me tightly. When they had finished, one spoke for the group when she said, "Dr. Gregory, you haven't changed a bit after all these years. Not one bit."

I'm not certain what she meant exactly by that lovely compliment, but I like to think she was saying to me — as she thought back on her time in our band, our Bicentennial Band, our travels and contests, and many other experiences over the years — something along the line of, "You haven't changed a bit in the way you see us. We were your students, and you cared for us, and you held us to a higher standard than most others did. You haven't changed a bit." At least that's what **I** heard her saying. But maybe, just maybe, she was saying something much less complicated, but even more profound as she remembered the bus lists for the Detroit trip. She simply could have meant..."You still look at us and see us...and we all look the same to you. You haven't changed a bit."

<u>Reminder</u>

Sometimes the lessons of hurt and disappointment cut less deeply when shared with someone close to you. Or in my case, shared with a group of 174 amazing young people who helped make my life richer and more meaningful. That special band trip was the reminder of those lessons I carry with me even today.

<u>*Lesson Take-Away:*</u> *We have students in our classrooms and people in our lives who bring hurt with them, because it is part of their lives. Many times what they need most is someone who cares for them for who they are and what they are. Students have very little control over the circumstances of their lives. Teachers can bring healing to hurt.*

Chapter Nine:
The Lesson of Loneliness

Betrayal

"For there to be betrayal, there would have to have been trust first."
— Suzanne Collins, The Hunger Games

The Hurt

She was an average clarinet player, not exceptionally strong, not exceptionally weak...just average. But she was a good band student. Always at rehearsals with her assignments seemingly prepared well enough to get by and not call attention to her playing abilities, or lack thereof. Just average. What was not shown or brought to class was the nightmare from her home life. That was kept private...mostly.

I think her quiet nature and passive personality when around other band members allowed her peers, and her director, to misunderstand those traits as evidence she was happy when she was involved socially with other band students. After all, given the right circumstances, band students can be a pretty active and sometimes boisterous group when enjoying the company of others. She seemed comfortable with her friends, if only from the edges of the social circles. Safe maybe...

During the early years of my teaching career when the demand for higher test scores and increased enrollment in advanced placement courses was not so critical, sometimes seniors who had an "open spot" in their class schedule could request to be a Teacher Aide for a specific teacher. I was fortunate to have one each semester for my planning period and sometimes for an additional class hour as well. My clarinet player was my planning period Teacher Aide during the second semester of her senior year. During this time her tragic betrayal came to light.

The primary purpose of a Teacher Aide was to assist a designated teacher with minor administrative duties and organizational activities of the teacher without placing the student in a position of dealing with confidential information of other students. My clarinet player was very efficient in helping with those things, but in the early spring of that year I noticed her becoming even quieter and seemingly more withdrawn from her peers. Not the actions of a senior who soon will be graduating from high school and heading to college for the next chapter in her young life.

Occasionally I would inquire of her as to how things were going with her last semester of classes or what plans she had for the summer as she prepared for college. Her answers were perfunctory, using as few words as possible to answer my questions without being rude or disrespectful. Things were "OK" or "All right" or "They're good," rather than complete responses. I met privately with the school counselor to ask for her guidance and she suggested I continue spending time visiting with my clarinet player since she apparently felt comfortable around me. Otherwise the student would not have requested to be my Teacher Aide. The counselor said she would speak with the student's other teachers to see if they had noticed changes in her behavior in their classes. We shared concern for this bright and capable young person who seemed to have lost her way.

One day during my planning period I was working on some tasks assigned by my local administration when I noticed my clarinet player was crying softly as she sat at her desk across the room. She wasn't trying to get my attention; in fact, she was attempting to hide her emotions. That wasn't working, so I asked if I could help her as she obviously was very upset about something. She once again tried the, "It'll be OK" answer, but this time I pressed the issue a bit further. This time she responded with, "Sometimes I feel like I'm alone and can't talk to anybody." Not so, I assured her. I was interested in all my students. She could talk with me, in confidence, and I would do my best to help, no matter what the situation. After a rather lengthy pause, she looked up, took a big breath, and said, "I'm involved with a married man."

Stunned would be a mild description of my reaction. There were many other words I could use, but let's stay with stunned for now. After some thought, I asked if she had told her mother. Absolutely not! Mom would "go crazy" if she knew. How about a close friend? Again, no. She was too embarrassed. The school counselor? Not happening as she didn't feel comfortable talking with someone she didn't know very well. My last resort...have you thought about talking with one of the pastors at your church? Long pause, deep breath, then the answer: "No, because one of them is the one I'm involved with. He took advantage of me while we were on a youth retreat." This was the point at which I had to revisit "stunned." It no longer carried the impact I felt.

I tried to gather my thoughts before speaking again, but my clarinet player seemed relieved to have spoken openly about her situation, so she continued her story. It seems "the event" had taken place the previous fall. Apparently, this "pastor" had been planning to take advantage of my clarinet player and had been arranging details of the retreat to best serve his perversion, or either he simply took advantage of a young woman in a setting where she felt she had no recourse or options other than to comply. After all, he was her "pastor." The more she talked about the horrible encounter the more her emotions came to the surface. Her crying became sobbing; her words that had been hesitant now came in a rush; the soft volume of her initial speech was now strong and with a harsh edge. Finally, she had found a release from the nightmare she had experienced at the hands of someone she trusted.

I asked her permission to speak confidentially with our school counselor and with my pastor, who also was a close personal friend of mine, so that I might be better equipped to offer her advice. She agreed and I promised to be very discreet and professional, not mentioning names, as I spoke with those whom I trusted. Hopefully, my clarinet player could find ways of dealing with this tragedy. Hopefully, this "pastor of young people" would be dealt with in a manner consistent with and appropriate to his betrayal and abuse of those in his charge for safekeeping.

I left the counseling and follow-up legal actions to those qualified to address such things. My concern was my clarinet player. She seemed "better" in the days and weeks following our talk as I carefully inquired how things were going. She seemed receptive to the idea of meeting with a professional counselor specifically trained in dealing with physical and emotional hurt of this nature and said she would "think about it." Possibly she was on the path toward healing.

I don't think she ever healed completely from the betrayal and subsequent abuse she suffered. Could <u>anyone</u>, especially a young person, go through something so traumatic, on so many levels, and ever be fully whole again? However, she did have a successful completion to her senior year and, as far as I know, her college years were good ones.

I didn't hear from her after she left high school, but I hoped she found ways of dealing with her betrayal and hurt as she moved through the healing process. I can't imagine ever completely recovering from such a horrific event. Still, I hoped she could use this tragedy as a means to become stronger rather than allowing it to destroy her life completely. Sometimes the wound truly is where the light enters.

As for the "youth pastor," I did not follow his demise, but I am confident every action was taken to provide appropriate punishment for his evil deeds and to ensure he never again would be in a position to render so much harm to someone else, especially to a young person. Once again, lesson taught; lesson learned. This one was full of hurt and evil.

<u>Reminder</u>

All of us come into contact with others who have hurt in their lives. Sometimes they are our students; sometimes they are our friends; other times they simply cross our path. May we always be aware of those who possibly are living with loneliness and be willing to be a presence in their lives.

"It is easier to forgive an enemy than to forgive a friend.
— William Blake

Alone

"The most terrible poverty is loneliness, and the feeling of being unloved."
— *Mother Teresa*

The Lost One

This young person was the quintessential "student who needs band more than the band needs the student." Being in the band, especially the marching band, apparently was the only true social life this student had. Her high school years were ones where she attached herself to a group, usually band people, and participated in the activity of their choosing. She never seemed to have much interest in initiating things...things such as conversations, ideas for outside school hours, making friends, or becoming better at playing her instrument.

She was a "follower," but there was something about her that gave me the impression she would really like to be recognized, possibly even celebrated for what she could do or simply for who she was. Maybe she was too quick to laugh at someone's joke, perhaps her laughter was a bit too enthusiastic or overdone, or maybe her body language asked too eagerly to be invited into someone else's life. That recognition never really happened, so she tried other ways.

Her "different" approach to being recognized was through her physical well-being. One day during marching band practice while we were checking a formation on the field, she passed out. Not an uncommon occurrence when working with a large number of high school students in an outside setting involving physical activity, but still one that brought significant attention to the person on the ground. Her friends gathered around her, the rehearsal was put on hold, someone ran to get water for her, and the attention of the entire group was focused on her as she recovered from the episode. Whether the passing out was intentional or accidental, the door was open for recognition she never before had received. It was the beginning of a long and sad journey.

Her "health issues" continued, even expanding into performance settings. There were times when she would "pass out" while standing on the sideline waiting to take the field for a halftime or contest marching performance, but she would "recover" in time to participate in the presentation. Each occurrence was a bit more dramatic than the last, either in length or in severity of fall. Obviously, there were issues that needed addressing.

I spoke with her parents regarding the situation, but they could provide no helpful information. They said they had taken her to their doctor, but he could find no physical reasons for the blackouts. No physical reasons implied other issues. Her desire for attention soon would lead to complex and dangerous situations, none of which was a good path to solutions.

The next level of "other issues" was that of physical abuse. She came to school one day with large bruises on her upper body, claiming she had been followed by men in a van. She said they caught her and physically assaulted her, leaving large and deep bruises. Once I was made aware of this situation, I immediately reported the abuse through our administrative and legal channels, hoping she would receive protection from her abusers. Police personnel, representatives from the local family and children services department, school officials, even fellow students were involved in helping to identify her abusers...without luck.

When no mysterious van or attackers could be located, attention was turned to the immediate family...one which had experienced a horrible tragedy less than a year earlier when their other child, my student's older brother, was murdered. The parents categorically and consistently denied any mistreatment of the daughter and the daughter, now eighteen years old, would not name them as abusers. It was a legal and administrative stalemate, but the physical abuse continued as did the stories of the van with men chasing her.

Her fellow students were concerned, to say the least, as they feared for her safety. There was a great deal of attention given to her by her band classmates, and her friends made certain, to the extent they could, she was not alone after school hours. The attention she so desperately wanted she now had. I guess the physical abuse, from wherever it came, seemed a small price to pay for the attention she so desperately craved and now was receiving from her peers. She was now one of the crowd. No! She was the center of attention and the most special one in the crowd. Mission accomplished.

It's not a huge leap from whatever she was experiencing and her subsequent actions to her becoming involved in the drug culture. Reports of her "running with the wrong crowd" came back to us after she graduated from high school. She did not attend college, instead opting to find employment in a store in the local shopping mall. The friends she had in high school and the attention she received from them were no longer there; she was once again alone in her world of loneliness, apparently willing to do whatever was needed to be accepted. My thought at the time: this was a tragic story waiting to be played out over what remained of her life.

No one seemed to know exactly what happened to this young woman after high school. She moved to another city not long after graduation, then another, eventually disappearing from the lives of those who had known her years before. Efforts to reach her for class reunions and other such "stay in touch" events never produced results. It was as if she no longer existed. I thought of her often those first few years, then less often as time passed. But she never completely left my memory. I had no way of checking on her and none of her high school band members knew where she was. Her parents were gone by this time so all ties with her home and past were severed. She was lost.

<u>Reminder</u>

For certain my lonely student was an extreme case, but in every classroom and in every social setting there are those who are also lonely. Simply because they are in a crowd or with a group does not mean they are not. One can be lonely both in a crowd as well as when alone.

A reunion of my former band students was organized on the 50th anniversary of my appointment as Director of Bands at that school. Hundreds were in attendance and many stories were told and re-told, this time with a bit more embellishment than probably was needed. But after all, five decades should allow for some journalistic liberties here and there.

Somewhere along the way someone mentioned the lonely young lady, wondering what had happened to her. No one knew for certain until one of the organizers of the event spoke up. She had researched past band members, addresses, contact information, as well as possible secondary contacts for those she couldn't reach. She spent a great deal of time researching the location of our lonely young lady, but the results she eventually found were not what she had hoped. As of the date of her inquiry, our lonely student's name showed up in the National Missing and Unidentified Persons System. Nothing had been heard from or of her for several years. At some point in time, she very likely would be declared deceased.

I was saddened to hear of her apparent demise. The more I thought of her tragic situation the more I realized the terrible and wonderful challenges teachers have when serving their students. There are lonely children in every classroom. A name in the national database for missing, unidentified, and unclaimed persons is yet another, even more desperate, way of listing a lonely and lost person.

"I'm not much but I'm all I have."
— *Philip K Dick, **<u>Martian Time-Slip</u>***

<u>Lesson Take-Away:</u> Loneliness is a dark place. We have students who come into our classrooms looking for a brighter place. Teachers must always be sensitive to the opportunities of bringing light to darkness and helping those in need. We have those opportunities each day.

Chapter Ten:
The Lesson of Struggling

The Faulty Valve

*"Rock bottom became the solid foundation on which I rebuilt my
life."*
—J.K. Rowling

Rehearsal was going pretty well...nothing great, nothing disastrous. Just OK. The usual problems and challenges present every day were back again that day. Two steps forward and one back. Eventually, we would get there, or close, but progress was slow and I was pushing the band pretty hard to achieve what I felt was within the reach of the ensemble. Pretty much the same agenda and lesson plan for every day in late spring: Make it better than it was yesterday.

Our rehearsals were times of focused and intentional work. The students knew our objectives, how to achieve them, and what it would take to realize them. Nowhere in that plan was a place for distractions that had nothing to do with rehearsal; there were enough of them already built into the rehearsal format. My position on individual disturbances was that they not only were a disruption to rehearsal, but they also were an infringement on the rights of others to learn and were an insult to the work ethic of fellow ensemble members. I suppose that's the reason the rattling of the faulty valve by one of my trumpet players was unusually distracting while I was rehearsing another section of the band on a particular passage.

I stopped my instruction and asked him to stop disrupting the class. He apologized and did as requested. But it wasn't long before the same problem arose again. This time I was even more firm, possibly aggressive, with my comments to him. I very clearly told him that should the issue of the noisy valve come up again during rehearsal, he would be asked to leave and not return. He did not have the right to interfere with the learning process of others. Message clearly sent; hopefully, clearly understood. Unfortunately, the latter half was not.

The third, and final, transgression occurred only minutes after the second reprimand. I was furious and immediately dismissed him from class with instructions to pack up his instrument, faulty valve and all, and wait for me in my office. This issue of intentional disruption of our ensemble rehearsal simply could not go unpunished. He was a senior band member and certainly should know what was expected of him as well as what would not be tolerated during rehearsals. In addition to being upset with this senior for his lack of personal discipline and disregard for fellow ensemble members, I was disappointed he would behave in such a manner as to be disrespectful to me after having been in my band for over three years. The meeting in my office was going to be a turning point. Little did I know how significant this turning point lesson would be for me.

Rehearsal ended, and I quickly headed to my office to confront the trumpet player, fully intent on letting him know how upset and disappointed I was, both with his behavior and with him personally. What I wasn't prepared for and hadn't expected was his response. When I entered my office and closed the door his first words as he began to cry (yes, my senior trumpet player was crying) were, "Mr. Gregory, I'm so sorry. I didn't mean to cause problems and for sure I didn't want to offend you personally." I was caught off guard and quickly had to regroup. My response, "OK. Tell me what's going on." What followed was a deeply moving lesson for yours truly in one of the struggles in the life of a teenager.

He proceeded to tell me his mother had died a little over a year and a half ago, early in his junior year of high school, but his dad had remarried within six months of her passing. Recently, a new baby had come into the picture as the newest addition to the family. My trumpet player with the faulty valve said that just a few days prior to this incident in rehearsal, he and his dad had had a terrible argument about the new family dynamics and his dad had told him to leave...to get out. He could make it on his own. He was eighteen and could find a place to live. He needed to move out so dad and his new wife, and the baby, could have the privacy they wanted for their new family.

I asked my student how and where he was living. He replied that he was working a few hours each day at a fast-food restaurant so he had food and a little spending money. I asked about his sleeping arrangements, and he paused as if he were embarrassed. When I asked again, he said he was sleeping in his car so he could come to band rehearsal every day. He said the band was the only good thing in his life at that time, and he just couldn't give it up. His words took away mine. I was silenced by the enormity of his personal struggle and humbled by his determination to be present for our rehearsals, regardless of the personal sacrifices and hardships he had to endure.

As I listened to this tragic story, one no teenager should have to face, the issue of the faulty valve, even the noise he made when trying to repair it, faded far into the background. No longer standing in my office was a troublemaker who was disrupting my rehearsal; now I saw one of the bravest young men I had ever known as he shared a very personal and private struggle. I wondered if I would have been strong enough to survive had these circumstances been mine a generation before.

<u>Reminder</u>

Every time I faced a class after that encounter, either in rehearsal or otherwise, I made certain to remind myself there were students in that room who were struggling. Students who were desperately searching for something to anchor their lives. Students who were confused as to what would happen to them day after day. Students who needed something to bring comfort and security to their young lives. Students who needed the assurance of being part of something that brought beauty and pleasure into their troubled existence.

Now, many years after the faulty valve incident, I still remind myself that every time I step onto the podium...every time, I have the chance to do something good in the life of another person. I make certain I remind myself that every ensemble I conduct possibly will have someone in it who is finding special meaning and purpose by being there. Lesson well taught; lesson certainly well learned.

The Walker

"Success is not measured by what you accomplish, but by the opposition you have encountered, and the courage with which you have maintained the struggle against overwhelming odds."
—*Orison Swett Marden*

I had no idea how she got to school, much less to band rehearsals. At that time in my life and career I was more focused on developing the very best program I could and, because I was in the early years of my tenure at my school, I was very much a stickler for guidelines and rules. Had I not been, I believed the program would never grow and become one of quality. I just "made the rules," and it was up to the students to find a way to comply. It was only after a special Lesson was taught to me did I come to the realization that every person is different and every situation is unique. The time was right for me to be taught some important things by one of my students, whom I later came to know as The Walker.

She was transferred to my school in the early 1970s as part of the Federal desegregation order for our school system. I was new to my school and new to all my students, as they were to me. My goal was to have a great band program and it was my responsibility to do the best I could for all my students, both the ones returning to my school and the ones newly reassigned to it. The Walker was one of the new band members, and she wanted the same thing as I did.

My Advanced Band met at 8:00 a.m. each morning for forty minutes before homeroom began. We met again at 11:00 for our full hour of rehearsal. This rehearsal schedule had been in place prior to my arrival and I simply continued the practice. What I had not counted on were the transportation problems the schedule caused for my newly assigned students. Virtually all the reassigned students rode school buses each day, but the buses didn't arrive until approximately 8:20, and that would not work. The Advanced Band students were required to be at the early rehearsal. If they could not, they could be a member of the Concert Band which met only during the school day.

By the end of the first few weeks of classes I assumed all the Advanced Band students had worked out their transportation details satisfactorily as everyone was present each day. Yes and no... or rather no and yes. What came to my attention was the fact that many students had private means of coming to rehearsals while a few others used public transportation to arrive close enough to the school to walk the final distance in order to be on time.

At the end of the school day on a Friday a few weeks into the school year, The Walker came to my office and asked if she could share with me some of the details of her morning trip to school each day. Of course I was interested in her story, but it was my understanding that everyone had found a way to make their situation work. She had not, and she was facing a very real crisis.

Her morning journey to school consisted of an early-morning city bus ride to a location several blocks from our school in an all-White neighborhood, something that was not uncommon many years ago in the South. She then had to walk the final distance regardless of weather conditions or other circumstances, some of which were extremely dangerous. She told me how she had to pass by one house where the owner kept a large and aggressive dog fenced in. If the homeowner saw her walking by, he would let the dog out of the fenced area allowing it to chase my student, causing her to have to run as fast as she could simply to escape the attack. When she told me of her plight, I knew something had to change, and I was the person who had to make it happen.

When The Walker had finished telling this frightening story, she had tears in her eyes as she asked me if there was any way she could continue to be in the band but not have to walk by the attack dog each morning. The band was the only place in school where tensions between Blacks and Whites did not exist, a place where she was accepted for who she was and what she was, the place where she found peace and security in an otherwise tumultuous environment. She loved and needed band in her life. My turn.

I told her to go home and talk with her mother and tell her of my proposed transportation arrangement. If she approved and The Walker was comfortable with it, we would begin the following Monday morning. I committed to leaving my house a good bit earlier than usual, driving to the other end of our city, meeting her at her apartment while her mother watched, and driving together back to our school, which was in the center of town, in time for the early rehearsal. I was always at my office by 7:15, so I met The Walker at 6:45 each morning. Problem solved.

Now...consider that situation in the context of the 21st century. Here I was, a twenty-four-year-old White male meeting a teenage Black girl each morning at her apartment then driving off with her in his car in order to travel across town for a band rehearsal. Absolutely no way that could work today! Imagine the liabilities involved! How about the potential for scandal with a teacher and a student in that situation, not considering race as a factor? But I never gave them a second thought, other than making certain her mother was comfortable with the arrangement. The transportation problems for The Walker were my main concern. Both she and Mom were thrilled and grateful.

Decades later after having served several years in an administrative position in the Superintendent's office of the school system where I worked, I realized just what an enormous risk I had taken in transporting a student to school each day in my personal vehicle. As I said, the arrangement The Walker, her mother, and I worked out was a one-time solution, but still one with significant liability. But again, liability and possible problems never occurred to me; I was just trying to work out a rehearsal attendance issue.

Years later at a reunion of band students from the early years of my teaching career, The Walker spoke of my intervention into her story, of how I was willing to do something for a person I did not know, how I took a risk by driving to her apartment every day (many times during the winter it would be completely dark when I met her), and how those acts of kindness and caring changed her life. She said I was willing to help someone I had known for only a short time while the White family for which her mom worked never offered assistance of any kind.

I never viewed it that way. I just wanted to have a really fine band, and she desperately wanted to be part of that program. All I needed to do was find a way to get her to the early rehearsal each morning. At the time, I thought less of the possible concerns with the transportation arrangement than I did with whether we would be able to be at my office by 7:15 every morning for me to unlock the band room. After all, traffic could be a nightmare some days, and being late was not a viable option.

The Lesson in Struggling was not made clear to me until many years later when The Walker and I were visiting and she told me she would never have made it through high school had it not been for being in our band. And she could not have been in the Advanced Band had I, as a twenty-four-year-old novice band director, not been willing to take risks in order to help save one of my students, a teenage girl.

Reminder

Some lessons are not learned completely without the passing of time. I still am amazed by the impact my actions had on that student's life, and I never realized it at the time. The Lesson of Struggling still reminds me there are those I teach and those with whom I associate who are dealing with unknown personal and professional struggles on a daily basis. Lesson very well learned.

"Life doesn't get easier or more forgiving; we get stronger and more resilient."
—Steve Maraboli

Lesson Take-Away: *A teacher's day is filled with opportunities to help those who struggle. Some students manage their challenges; some students come to us feeling they are overburdened with their struggles. Helping those students is part of our calling...it is our nature and purpose.*

Chapter Eleven:
The Lesson of Commitment

The Rehearsal

"We are what we repeatedly do. Excellence, then, is not an act, but a habit."
— Aristotle

Springtime in the South brings many things: new plant growth, warmer weather, the promise of new beginnings, pollen...and a fairly regular appearance of afternoon thunderstorms. Early April had all of those this particular year, my first year as Director of Bands at a small university in north Georgia. The band program, what there was of it, was very small but with potential for growth and better days to come. My first rehearsal of the fall semester with the band (there was only one and not much of one at all) had thirteen college students on roll and in attendance. Present also were some community members who in past years had been invited to play with the ensemble as the music department operated as a bit of a "town and gown" collaboration.

On this particular afternoon a rather large thunderstorm, one of those strong but not long-lasting, rolled through our area, leaving behind large areas with power outages. Our campus was one of those places and immediately the word came from the Office of the University President that all afternoon and evening classes were cancelled. Not good news for my little band, which by this time in the second semester had grown to nearly forty members...thirty-eight to be exact. I didn't have any choice but to send that information to the band students, by whatever means possible. My message was that during our rehearsal time (we rehearsed Mondays and Wednesdays from 4:00 until 5:15), we would meet with anyone who was interested and could come to the rehearsal room. Possibly we could have sectionals, or small group instruction, or even some sort of private instruction, or something...

This one was going to be interesting. A main point of focus for our ensemble that semester had been that of committing to the process of becoming better and of following through with those things that would help us reach our goals. But I'll have to admit, the closer time came for rehearsal to begin, the more apprehensive I became, and the less certain

I was about what would take place at 4:00 o'clock. There were several students milling about the rehearsal area. Some were playing their instruments; others were socializing...but they were there. In my somewhat innocent and fantasy-like thoughts, I was hoping there would be at least enough students show up to have some variation of a rehearsal or practice session.

As we well know, college students very seldom will turn down an opportunity to miss class, especially if there is no penalty. The announcement from the university president gave them a "hall pass" from afternoon class responsibilities, so there were music students roaming the halls of the Fine Arts Building, thoroughly enjoying some slack time without fear of penalty or reprisal from the instructor. Several of the students had gathered in my office, and we were having a bit of an impromptu class on, as they liked to say, "Things and Stuff." I'm comfortable doing "Things and Stuff."

Shortly before 4:00, I dismissed the impromptu class with instructions to get out their instruments and move to the rehearsal room. Still, I had hopes that we would have a decent number show up. There had been students in the rehearsal room for an hour or so practicing or working on their private studio assignments, so I knew we would have at least <u>some</u> students present. And we did.

I walked into the band room just before the appointed time for rehearsal to begin and was surprised to find students <u>not</u> preparing for sectionals. Nothing like that. Seated and ready to begin rehearsal at 4:00 o'clock, as we did twice each week, were thirty-eight band members. **All thirty-eight were there!** Not one person had chosen to skip rehearsal. For the first time, but certainly not the last, I was amazed by these men and women.

That day our program, our very new and fledgling program, took a direction that would lead to future successes. That was the day I would name in later years as the turning point for our band. Thirty-eight decisions were made that afternoon and our program was changed. To borrow the title from Malcolm Gladwell's remarkable book, that day for us was the essence of "The Tipping Point."

They had chosen to come to rehearsal, possibly because they had heard me say many times, "There is never enough rehearsal time." That, or maybe, "You can't make up a missed rehearsal." Could even have been, "As an individual, you have a responsibility to the group. Our rehearsals and performances are some of the few times in your academic career where your individual actions will affect the success of others." Possibly my university students were in fact listening to some of the things I said in rehearsal...possibly.

Whatever the case, that afternoon following an April thunderstorm which shut down power across our campus and cancelled classes, all my band students showed up to rehearse (power was restored eventually, but that ship had sailed and there would be no reinstatement of classes that day once the president had cancelled all university activities). They didn't have to be there; they chose to be there. That day, that muggy April afternoon, the direction of the band program at my little university changed for the better. There now had been a visible demonstration of the commitment from those men and women...one that would move us forward and allow us to make exponential progress in our music making and in our teacher preparation programs.

<u>Reminder</u>

That wonderful rehearsal experience, and it truly was an exceptional time, remains as one of my favorite memories of my years at that university. As I look back on the successes we achieved and the life-changing experiences we shared, my thoughts always come back to that one afternoon when thirty-eight students renewed my faith in the potential of musical ensembles when a shared commitment is acted upon. Once again, I was reminded that a commitment is a choice we make every day, over and over. For certain...

More, Please...

"Commitment is an act, not a word."
— Jean-Paul Sartre

I was enjoying the beginning of the year at my little university where we had begun a band program eight years before. Rehearsals were going well, students were working hard, we had experienced considerable success in attaining goals, our enrollment was up (from thirteen college students at my first rehearsal to approximately ninety at that time), and the performance ability level of the ensemble had risen significantly. I was excited about the possibilities the year held.

We were at the rehearsal and performance levels where we could present two formal concerts plus a departmental-wide seasonal concert series the first semester, and two formal concerts in the spring semester. Every concert was performed to a full house and our seasonal concerts, the only ones where admission was charged, were sold out (note: five seasonal concerts were presented in four days). I was enjoying our work and was pleased with the progress we were making. It was around this time that a group of senior band members and section leaders came into my office after one of our two weekly rehearsals. They asked if they could "talk with me." Most of the time, such things raise caution flags with me. This one did also, but I misread their message.

Their question for me was whether we could have an additional, smaller, more select ensemble, chosen from the large Symphonic Band. The larger group with some ninety members did not, in the opinion of this group of student leaders, allow for the exploration and performance of some of the more difficult music in our band repertoire because of the disparity in individual ability levels among ensemble members.

More advanced and demanding music could be read and performed with a smaller, more skilled ensemble. The smaller ensemble would be comprised of the top players in each section, bringing the total number of players in the new group to somewhere in the vicinity of fifty instrumentalists. I was confused. Were they asking for <u>more</u> rehearsal time? My first reaction was to explain to them there were no more "rehearsal slots" available for ensembles. Their response: "Not really. We've thought about that."

Our School of Music, because of our smaller overall enrollment numbers compared to larger state universities, had an assigned rehearsal time for each major ensemble, one not in conflict with another. I told the students of these assignments and explained there were few, if any, large ensemble rehearsal times available.

A reason we avoided rehearsal schedule conflicts was that many of our students performed in several ensembles. We encouraged our instrumentalists to sing in one of the choirs, our wind players rotated into and out of orchestra participation, and Jazz Band members performed in and with Symphonic Band and Concert Choirs. It was our philosophy that we should allow, and encourage, students to broaden their musical understandings by participating in as many major ensembles as possible.

My explanation of limited rehearsal time assignments and the very likely possibility there was not one available for the new ensemble was met with, "We've thought about that, and we've found a time...Wednesday evening after we finish band rehearsal." They wanted _more rehearsals?_ University men and women were asking for more class time and added responsibilities? Could that be a possibility? If so, _why_ did they want more work? Couldn't be for more course credit; they would receive none. It was completely extra.

The students had checked schedules and found an unclaimed block of time in the rehearsal room, and they wanted it. They had taken a poll with band members and found unanimous agreement for the added ensemble and the extra rehearsal time. Everyone understood how the logistics would work on Wednesdays: band rehearsal from 4:00 until 5:15, quick dinner break, and back to smaller ensemble rehearsal from 6:00 until 8:00. Had these college students, ones I thought to be smart and insightful, lost their reasoning abilities? Certainly no one in their situation would be asking for additional time commitments and more responsibilities...would they? Apparently so.

My position, should I agree to their proposal, was there could be no absences from these Wednesday night sessions and ensemble members would come to rehearsals prepared to rehearse, not practice. The music would be more demanding and our rehearsal time would be inversely proportional to those demands...more results with less preparation time.

"No problem," they said. They already had complete agreement from everyone on this part. As they explained, it went without saying I would be uncompromising with the attendance part. They understood. After all, band rehearsals were the only class where students never considered skipping. It wasn't an option. Sounded as if they really did want, "more, please."

I told them I would consider their request and bring their proposal to the Dean. Hopefully I would have an answer for them in a day or so, certainly before the end of the week. After due consideration and with the approval of the Dean, I agreed to start the new ensemble.

The students were thrilled! I met with the student leaders again and discussed procedural details of the newly formed ensemble in order for our rehearsals to begin the following week. Long day on Wednesdays for yours truly, but what conductor could turn down a request such as this one? Not me.

The inaugural rehearsal of what the students wanted to call the "Chamber Winds" was a huge success. I had packed the music folder with even more challenging music, all of which required a new level of rehearsing from everyone. For the most part, the group could sight-read the selections and seemed thrilled to be involved with that level of literature. After the first rehearsal, there was obvious excitement among the members of the ensemble, never mind they had been playing their instruments since 4:00 pm with only a short break for recovery and a quick dinner. They were pleased with what they had done and were ready to take on the next challenges. I could provide them with those.

The first concert of the Chamber Winds was in November and the program was shared with the Symphonic Band. Two complete programs, one with approximately ninety players and one with fifty-four. Different program formats and different levels of literature, but both with listeners as well as performers in mind. Audience ears and artist ears–very important to keep both in mind when performing for our patrons. Parenthetically, in my opinion, that premise seems to be ignored with many university band concerts, hence one of the reasons for the decline in attendance for live concerts, or even for concerts that are live streamed. Just my thoughts.

I explained to the audience at the initial concert of the Chamber Winds how the ensemble had come into being. Again, I stressed the point that the students came to me, asking for more rehearsals. More responsibilities, more demands on their time from an already busy schedule, and greater musical challenges with literature choices. They had <u>asked</u> for those! The students actually were asking me to give them more work and to ask more from them. As I said, it was not the first, nor last, time these students would surprise me in a delightful and rewarding way.

This special group of men and women, and their insistence on having an additional, more advanced ensemble, had given our program the chance to experience performance opportunities realized by very few others. Our Chamber Winds received an invitation to perform for the annual Georgia Music Educators Association Inservice Conference, and an invitation was extended to us from the prestigious American Bandmasters Association to perform for their national convention, one given to only four or five bands each year. Remarkable achievements...and with only one rehearsal a week. No exceptions. Remarkable indeed...

These accomplishments would not have been realized had that handful of students, those special men and women so very dedicated to our art form, not come to me with the crazy idea of asking for more rehearsals and more demands on their already full schedules. Just leave it to band kids to surprise you when you are least expecting it, and with a request you would never have imagined. Was I the lucky one or what? Had I actually found a group of university women and men who wanted more and better things? I think I had.

That special meeting, their request, the ensemble commitment, the musical results we produced together...those were things I tucked away in my special memory files to remind me once again of the compelling beauty of music and how it changes lives. A "can we talk" meeting doesn't necessarily have to raise a caution flag; sometimes the flag can represent something great is about to begin. Trust me on this one...some "talks" definitely are worth it. Just leave it to band kids to surprise us in ways we had not imagined.

<u>Reminder</u>

Sometimes our students will surprise us with unusually wonderful things. Sometimes they will fail to meet our expectations. Sometimes they will exceed what we ask of them. At times they will disappoint us. Other times they will thrill us with their accomplishments. Sometimes they will frustrate us. Or they will be our inspiration. They will ask much of us. They will give much to us. But at all times they will be drawn to excellence, and they will show us how to be better teachers...they will teach us.

"It always seems impossible until it's done"
— Nelson Mandela

<u>Lesson Take-Away:</u> A commitment is a choice we make every day, day after day. Our students see our commitment through the things we do for and with them. They know whether ours is sincere or one of pretense. It is our choice. They learn commitment through us.

Chapter Twelve:
The Lesson of Humor...Revisited

The Conductor in Italy

"Why do you always insist on playing when I'm trying to conduct?"
— Eugene Ormandy

The National Band Association undertook a new and innovative project during the early 2000s in an effort to spotlight exceptional young conductors in conjunction with our international NBA members in Europe. The National Band Association's "International Conductor's Symposium" was created and the inaugural event was held in Rome, Italy with La Banda dell'Esercito (the Italian Army Band). Maestro Fulvio Creux was the Director of that exceptional ensemble.

Invitations to audition for selection were sent to NBA members across the United States and "young conductors" (those 35 years old or younger) were encouraged to apply for acceptance. Three conductors would be chosen and would travel to Rome for a week-long event of conducting, score study, private instruction, and a grand finale concert with the Italian Army Band. It would be a tremendous honor to be chosen to participate, and winners would have an opportunity to study and conduct in a city and country rich in the history and heritage of Western music.

Three conductors were chosen from the nation-wide audition process and they, along with three NBA Past Presidents who would serve as tutors/mentors for the workshop, headed to Rome for the week of work with a fantastic band of professional musicians in one of the most beautiful and historic countries in the world. It was going to be a fantastic learning experience for all involved. The conductors would face the challenge of rehearsing a band whose members spoke a language different from theirs; they would be expected to communicate their musical and artistic rehearsal instructions to the ensemble primarily through their conducting gestures. Speaking of a "learning curve..."

The mentors/tutors worked with and advised the conductors as to literature choices for the rehearsals and the grand finale concert, encouraging them to choose selections representative of quality compositions from our American repertoire for the concert. Two of the conductors named well-known works from our standard literature for their work, but one conductor wanted to rehearse a famous Italian overture composed by Giacomo Puccini.

The conductor was cautioned about rehearsing and performing this particular selection...an Italian overture composed by an Italian composer in the country from which it came. Not to mention the fact that members of this professional ensemble of Italian musicians very likely had performed the composition many times, were familiar with the lyrics and plot of the opera, and had worked with many skilled conductors over the years. This overture was part of the "musical DNA" of those musicians. What could the American conductor bring to yet another performance of this work? In spite of our counsel, the young conductor said he "really wanted to do this piece." Said it was one of his "favorites." So be it...he had been forewarned.

Somewhere mid-week of the rehearsals the conductors were deeply involved with preparations of their work, most of which were going well. Still, the conductor of the Italian overture was struggling...as was predicted and pretty much expected by the mentors. He was "flailing away" on the podium with exaggerated gestures and movements that had very little connection to the music being played. Head in the score and arms waving above his head he was "working hard and going nowhere." That was the moment in time when clarity was brought to a somewhat murky situation through a simple question.

The principal clarinetist (comparable to the concert master of an orchestra) got up from his seat and walked to where I was standing, taking rehearsal notes while the band was playing. He leaned toward me and quietly said, **"David, why does this conductor argue with the music?"** His question brought a chuckle from me at first as I thought he meant it as humorous. Not so. That was when I realized his was a statement so simple yet brilliantly insightful...why <u>was</u> the conductor <u>arguing</u> with the music rather than listening to what it had to say? I had no idea.

I didn't share the exact words of the principal clarinetist with the conductor as he would have been even more discouraged (he had sufficient challenges with the music already). I did, however, offer some thoughts and suggestions as to ways he might better navigate some of the more difficult passages and better achieve his goals. But the question has stayed with me over the years as I have witnessed conductors in rehearsals and performances who very much seemed to be "arguing with the music."

As I reflect on my conducting work with many ensembles and in many different settings, I suspect there have been a number of times (probably many more than I would like to admit) when I was "arguing with" rather than listening carefully to what the music was implying and what it was "trying to say." The words of my Italian friend still sound in my mind every time I step onto the podium. Thank you for reminding me, in a somewhat humorous manner, to listen and hear and see things more clearly.

<u>Reminder</u>

The light-hearted lesson of conducting practices with our "young" conductor reminded me of the many opportunities we have in our classrooms, whatever form those rooms may take, to listen to what is being implied rather than always assuming what we think should be said. Sometimes it is in fact the music with which we "argue." Other times it might be a student who has a message or need, but possibly we are too focused on what we believe to be the right answer to hear what the student is trying to say. May we always strive not to "argue with our music" but rather be receptive to what truly is being said.

"Listening is a complete act; the very act of listening brings its own freedom."
— Krisnamurti, <u>"Commentaries on Living 2"</u>

The Concert

"What to do about the cannon shots?" Anyone who has programmed Peter Ilyich Tchaikovsky's "1812 Overture" has had to deal with that question. If the concert is outside, does the conductor try to arrange for weapons using blank ammunition or does she/he simply add large percussion battery instruments and hope the audience members are not expecting actual cannons to sound off at the appropriate times? If the concert is inside, how best to come up with something that would give audience members the impression of heavy artillery at the grand finale section of the composition?

Such is the dilemma of every director who has programmed this selection...unless you are fortunate enough to stand before one of our amazing United States Military Bands, who when programming the work outside can actually have cannons fired (with blanks) from a distance...on cue. Military bands performing the piece inside can still provide very creative ways of giving audience members realistic sound effects, not necessarily so with high school bands and inside concerts.

The grand finale to my spring concert that year was, you guessed it: "1812 Overture." The students were excited because virtually every one of them was familiar with the selection but had never performed it. To have the opportunity of performing the piece, with cannon effects, was certainly going to be a highlight of the year, if not their high school band career. Things were moving along nicely and, for the most part, the technical aspects of the concert were coming along well. The cannon effects still were a work in progress and a number of ideas were being considered.

Finally, after considerable research, input from students, guidance from the school administration, and approval from the Superintendent's office the decision was made to use target pistols with blank cartridges fired into an empty fifty-five-gallon barrel backstage in the percussion section. With careful monitoring from another music faculty member, trial runs were conducted during rehearsals and things seemed to be on track for a memorable finale to our concert season. What I didn't know was just how memorable this particular concert would be.

The week of our concert I invited Colonel Hal Gibson to drop by one of our rehearsals and give us feedback and share his insights with us. He was the recently retired Commander and Conductor of the United States Army Field Band, the position from which he was chosen by the Pentagon and named as the Commander and Conductor of the United States Armed Forces Bicentennial Band, an elite ensemble comprised of top players from the five major service bands in Washington, D.C.

That all-star, professional band presented concerts in every state in our country during the year of our national Bicentennial Celebration and performed for hundreds of thousands of concertgoers. Upon completion of a magnificent year of performances with that ensemble, Colonel Gibson retired from the United States Army and subsequently was named Director of Bands at Columbus College, an institution whose campus was very near our school. As always, he was very appreciative of our invitation and graciously agreed to visit with us. Our students were thrilled to have him in our rehearsal once again. His visit was the catalyst...

While he talked about the Tchaikovsky selection, he shared some of his experiences with his performances of the piece with various military bands he had conducted and with the professional orchestra of which he had been a member. Of particular interest to my students was the event where he described a practical joke played on the person responsible for firing blanks from a handgun into a barrel...an arrangement very similar to the one we were using.

He shared the story of how the percussion section leader of the orchestra in which he was playing came to the conductor just before he took the stage to begin the selection and told him someone had poured several bags of baking flour into the barrel where the blanks were to be fired. With no time to undo the prank, the conductor took the stage for the grand finale.

When time came for the cannon effects, the musician assigned the "cannon duty" stood at attention and, on cue, fired into the barrel. The result was a cloud of white powder exploding from the container with each shot, very similar to the smoke that would discharge from a cannon firing. To the audience members, those actions seemed to achieve the desired effect, but to the musicians, not so much.

When the selection was finished and the applause was filling the concert hall, the conductor looked back to the percussion section and there, standing smartly at attention, was the "cannon effect" person covered in white powder. The upper half of his otherwise immaculate concert uniform was covered in snow-white flour, and his face, including his glasses, had a ghostly pale covering that was interrupted only slightly when he exhaled his breath.

As this story was being told, I sensed an unusual interest level from some of my students as they exchanged furtive glances and smiles. Once Colonel Gibson had left and I returned to the podium, the first thing I said to my ensemble was, "Don't even think about it. Don't. Even. Think. About It." Believing the issue had been addressed and settled, we continued the rehearsal in preparation for our concert later that week.

After our final rehearsal on concert day, just as a precautionary measure, I called our Property Manager into my office and gave him specific and exceptionally clear instructions pertaining to the barrel and our concert. I told him he was to allow no one, NO ONE, near the barrel before the concert. We set the stage following our last rehearsal and I once again reminded him not to leave the barrel unattended. He assured me he would not allow anyone to put flour into the barrel. I locked the hall and headed home to change and prepare for the evening's event. This young man, who was Property Manager, was a delightful and capable person, and I trusted him to protect our set-up. And he did.

I had asked our orchestra teacher to assist with our concert and he was excited to be part of the program. He was responsible for firing the blanks from the handgun into the barrel, one of the conditions of approval from our administration, so as not to have a student be involved with that part. On the day of the concert, I shared with him the "flour in the barrel" story and told him what steps I had taken to prevent something similar from happening during our program. We were confident the program would go without a hitch...other than the usual technical, tone, and intonation peccadilloes that were constant companions. As I said earlier, this was going to be a memorable concert...one we would long remember because we programmed "1812 Overture," with cannon effects.

As usual, I arrived quite a bit early for the program and found our Property Manager sitting on stage diligently guarding the set-up, not allowing anyone to be near the "1812 Barrel." I worked on last-minute details such as program distribution, lighting crew instructions, double-checking recording details, and doing my best to solve or ignore last minute crises of band members. During this backstage mass of teenage, pre-concert confusion our orchestra teacher rushed into my office with his news: someone had emptied several bags of flour into the barrel.

I was furious and immediately called our Property Manager into my office. When he arrived, I gave him a reprimand with both barrels (so to speak) regarding my instructions, his responsibilities, the impact on our concert, and any other pertinent topics I could think of. To bring my scolding to a close I reminded him I had told him, implicitly, that he was to allow NO ONE near our barrel before the concert. After a slight pause, he spoke quietly, and with a certain degree of remorse, when he said, "I did exactly what you told me to do. I didn't let anyone get near it." How then did this happen? How did flour get into the barrel? He said again, after an even longer pause, "I did it. I put the flour in the barrel."

He had followed my instructions to the letter. I couldn't fault him there, so I tried to appeal to his sense of responsibility as a leader in the band, however, without much success. He said he would try to remove the flour but all three of us knew that was not a viable option, so our orchestra teacher said he would handle the situation. I had other things to worry about so I agreed.

The orchestra teacher returned to my office just before the beginning of the concert to say he had taken care of the problem...he had poured water into the barrel to prevent flour dust and had placed wet paper music folios on top of the flour. There would be no explosion of white powder during the cannon shots. Things should be fine, and I could focus on the rest of the concert. I should have thought about this situation more but I had other things to think about and other small fires to put out before concert time. Two bands, two full concerts, a student conductor, a student teacher, and only one director in charge.

Time came for the Symphonic Band to perform, and the stage was set. Black curtains surrounded the stage. Ladies were dressed in formal black dresses, men in tuxedos, the director in his formal attire...wet flour with a paper covering in the barrel. We were ready for "1812 Overture."

Unknown to me at the time, most of the band members were in the know regarding the barrel situation. Some of the seniors had approached the principal and explained the scenario, assuring him they would make certain there would be no issues with damage to the facility, and they would help clean the stage after the performance. He thought it would be a great way to end the concert. He loved the joke, especially when he heard the backstory of the military band leader and his exploits with the flour...and I thought my principal was a friend of mine who supported me and encouraged my work.

When the big moment came in the overture for the cannon shots, our orchestra teacher dutifully fired the handgun into the barrel of wet flour, which by now had turned into a thick paste, probably ready for an oven, and the wet paper folios tore apart immediately upon the firing of the blanks. When the first cannon shot rang out, on cue, white paste erupted from the barrel and pieces of music folios sailed across and into the band. Band members continued playing as if this were part of our rehearsed procedure, even as subsequent cannon shots produced additional paper and paste detritus across the stage.

Audience members, thinking this display was a planned part of the cannon effect, loved every minute of it. All I could do was to continue conducting as I watched trumpet and clarinet players seated near "the cannon" become victims of the paste blasts. In spite of all that was happening during this chaos, everyone (with the possible exception of the conductor and the shooter of the pistol) was having a grand time.

After the concert, one of the parents came to me to say he did not remember any concert he had enjoyed more than this one, mainly because of the "great" cannon effects. He said he knew school officials probably would be upset because the black stage curtains now were splashed with flour paste, but he said he would personally pay to have them cleaned. Such an enjoyable concert, he said. It was one of his most memorable. One of mine too.

<u>The Wrap-up</u>

After the concert, most of the audience had left the hall, and the students were nearly finished storing their equipment. At the same time, our Property Manager and other officers (plus some parent volunteers) were busy cleaning the stage and removing paste from equipment. I was in my office reviewing the program and thinking about how the evening had gone when our orchestra teacher showed up, standing at my office door, a sight such as I had never before seen.

He had flour paste on his clothes, in his hair, on his face, matted in his large beard, and dripping from his glasses. I said nothing as I didn't know whether to laugh or be upset. He helped by smiling a paste-covered smile and saying, "Well, at least we didn't have white powder dust everywhere. The water and wet paper took care of that problem. Maybe next time we should plan a pizza party after the concert, and we could make our own pizza crust. We'll already have the dough.

As I said, it was one of the most memorable concerts ever. Funny now, but not so much then.

"The secret to humor is surprise"
— Aristotle

Some Laughs We Almost Missed

The Trombone Singer

A vocal performance/music education major at my university who had completed her Brass Methods Class requirements on trombone came into my office to ask if it would be possible for her to play in our concert band. We chatted for a while and came up with an arrangement that would work. She was excited; I was intrigued.

Not many rehearsals later, the vocal/trombone student came into my office in a state of more-than-moderate frustration. She said the hardest thing about playing in a band versus singing in a choir was the fact that in band she had to count rests. And that was hard to do!

She explained that when singing with the choir, each member had a full score. No need for counting rests; just follow the score and sing your part as indicated. She was <u>really</u> struggling with the concept of counting multiple measures of rests in band rehearsal. She had never had to do the "rest thing," and now here she was, a twenty-year-old music major facing a significant dilemma. I suspect, however, her struggle was heightened, rather than lessened, by some other members of the trombone section seated near her when they would "help" her count rests and then, for some inexplicable reason, lose count and have to start over.

She said she could sing and she could play. She just didn't understand why those rest things had to be so hard. Why couldn't playing in the band be less complicated. I must admit, sometimes I have those same thoughts.

The Beginning Clarinet Student With A Crisis

A band director friend of mine shared with me the story of one of her sixth grade beginning band clarinet students who came to her one day before class, early in the school year, with her mouthpiece ligature bent severely out of shape.

The young student, not able to remember the word "ligature" but remembering it had something to do with the clarinet mouthpiece and how it helped hold the reed in place, said to the director in a voice filled with frustration, "Somebody stepped on my embouchure!" (FYI for non-band people: the embouchure is the formation of the mouth while playing an instrument; the ligature for a clarinet is the device that holds the reed in place on the mouthpiece.)

Close enough. The director helped the young student repair her "embouchure" and all was good in the student's world once again.

The "Successful" Audition

I was on the audition panel for a district honor band event and my assignment was to listen to the low woodwinds: saxophones, bass clarinets, contra clarinets, and bassoons. During the bass clarinet auditions I discovered yet another way to navigate the scale requirements.

A young lady came into the audition room, seemingly well prepared for her time with the judging panel. We asked her to play her C Major scale; she played her F Major scale, quite well. We asked her to play her F Major scale, same scale again. We asked for her Bb scale, again her F Major. One last request: her D scale; you guessed it...F Major again.

We thanked her and then asked her to play her chromatic scale the range of her instrument. Her question, "Which chromatic scale do you want me to play?" Our response, "You choose your favorite one, and that'll be fine." She began playing on a note near the bottom of the range of her instrument (guess which note...F) and proceeded to move upward, sometimes chromatically, sometimes diatonically, but generally with average technical ability. When she "finished" her interpretation of the "chromatic scale," she sat back in her chair and nodded to the judging panel as if to indicate, "Well, that's it. I've done about all I can do with the scale part of the audition. Let's move on." Indeed, we did.

We thanked her for her audition, which, in its own strange way, was one she had prepared reasonably well, for the most part; it was just incorrect. Lesson: Practice doesn't necessarily make one better unless one is practicing the correct things correctly.

Washing the Mouthpiece

Every teacher who has taught beginning band understands the importance of teaching students to keep their instruments clean and in good playing condition, especially the woodwind mouthpieces. I scheduled weekly instrument inspections with my beginning classes just to make certain the instruments were in fact clean, and also to help students make instrument care a regular part of their practice and performance routines.

I instructed clarinet and saxophone players to wash their mouthpieces (which were made of hard rubber) in warm, not hot, soapy water, rinse them thoroughly, and dry them with a soft cloth at least one a week. After all, food particles and such will collect and establish residence inside a mouthpiece when it is played often and not cleaned regularly.

One day, a student brought his clarinet mouthpiece to me. Well, it resembled a mouthpiece. He related how he told his mom to wash the mouthpiece in hot, soapy water (note above instruction) and then dry it. Mom wanted to make certain all the germs were killed, so she placed the mouthpiece in boiling water and left it there for several minutes.

The finished product resembled a clarinet mouthpiece only when significant imagination was used. I could tell it once had been a mouthpiece, but those days were gone.

I found another mouthpiece for the young man to use and wrote a note to mom, thanking her for her extra care of the first mouthpiece, but asking that future cleanings involved only warm, not hot, water.

Apparently, some lessons are learned only when they are boiled down to their very essence (sorry). Such was the case with this former mouthpiece.

A Successful Finish to the Rehearsal

I had the good fortune to serve as conductor of a very fine adult community band for several years. During that time, we presented concerts for conventions, honor band events, pops concerts, and highly successful seasonal programs. This chuckle came from one of our holiday concerts.

The concert was scheduled for a Saturday evening, and a huge audience was expected. That afternoon we had our dress rehearsal with soloists, choirs, and guest conductors. The rehearsal was from 2:30 until 5:00 and the concert was to begin at 7:30.

Rehearsal went very well, and we took our dinner break before concert call time a couple of hours later. When we returned to the stage for the performance, one of our bass clarinet players was missing. No one seemed to know where she was; no one had seen her since the rehearsal ended.

Just before concert time, one of her section members called her to see if she was ok or if something had happened to her. When the bass clarinet player answered, all was good. The caller then asked her where she was as concert time was only five minutes away. Silence on the other end of the call...complete silence for many seconds.

Then..."I forgot about the concert. I was so excited with our great rehearsal, I just walked to my car, got in it, and drove home. The concert never crossed my mind...and I live an hour away from the performance site and can't make it back in time. I'm terribly embarrassed. Please tell Dr. Gregory I'm not absent-minded. I just forgot the concert."

Imagine her next rehearsal with our group. Even better, imagine her reaction when one of her students forgot an important deadline. Sometimes adult learning can be the most difficult. She really was a very fine teacher and band member. Still...

The Scale Specialist

It was that time again...time for scale pass-offs for our band techniques class, a class for those students who had switched to a new instrument or those who needed significant remedial work in order to rehearse and perform at the high school level.

This one young man came in to play his three required scales on his new instrument: the Bb, C, and F majors. He recently had switched from trumpet to French horn...the instrument he said he had always wanted to play. This was his first time to have an individual playing requirement on his French horn and he was quite nervous. I chatted with him for a bit before asking him to play, hoping he could relax. No luck there.

First, I asked for his C Major scale and he did an admirable job. Next was his Bb Major, and it was a bit of a struggle. His F Major scale was the most demanding of the three for an inexperienced player, and he did not do well at all on that one.

When he finished playing the F scale (and I am being generous with the term "finished playing the scale"), I jokingly said to him, "Was that your F scale or the Richter scale?" He hesitated for a few seconds and then said, "Well, it was supposed to be the F scale. I didn't know I had to prepare the other one."

Realizing he was still overcome with nervousness, I just said to him, "You're right. You only had to play three scales today. Thanks for preparing them. Keep on working hard."

To this day, I am intrigued as to what he would have attempted had I asked him to give the Richter scale a try. Who knows?

"I believe that the ability to laugh at oneself is fundamental to the resiliency of the human spirit."
*— Jill Conner Browne, **The Sweet Potato Queens' Big-Ass Cookbook***

Lesson Take-Away: Reminder...Laughter does not make us less of a teacher; it makes us more of a human.

Chapter Thirteen:
The Lesson of the Beauty of Music

The Conductor and His Dad

"If you play music with passion love and honesty, then it will nourish your soul, and heal your wounds and make your life worth living."
— Sting

The assignment for the Graduate Conducting class was pretty straightforward and not terribly difficult: choose a selection from the list of titles being prepared by the graduate class "conducting band" and be ready to conduct that piece on your assigned day. Each graduate student would have approximately ten minutes to rehearse and then conduct the chosen work. All the selections were of moderate technical difficulty as the rehearsal band was capable of performing only at that level. The class was not designed nor intended to be one of ensemble performance; it was a rehearsal setting that would allow each conducting student to receive feedback from the instructor specific to the student's demonstrated effectiveness on the podium.

This one conductor, a quite talented and capable podium presence, chose Frank Ticheli's "Earth Song" as his selection for evaluation. A beautifully crafted piece, one which would allow for and encourage expressive interpretation and musical phrasing, this selection was an ideal choice for this young conductor. Ensemble members and conductor alike were drawn to this piece as one that gave them musical rewards not offered in every composition for concert band.

The members of the rehearsal band enjoyed playing this piece and "The Conductor" named it as one of his favorite works for band in today's repertoire. Dr. Ticheli's skillful use of the beauty of dissonance and the simplicity of melodic line made this selection one filled with musical and artistic possibilities.

Time came for "The Conductor" to take the podium and rehearse the ensemble. He had done a thorough and accurate score study, and he knew what he wanted to achieve and how to reach those goals. The ensemble members were excited to perform this work and were ready for "The Conductor" to demonstrate his musicianship as together they rehearsed "Earth Song." This one had the potential of being a highlight of the week's work.

As expected, "The Conductor" did a beautiful job of shaping phrases, creating beautiful rubato sections as the music implied, allowing the ebb and flow of the musical lines to complement one another, finding ways to express musical nuance within the notes, and using both soft and strong dissonances to enhance the consonance the listener sought. It was a beautiful performance, one enjoyed by conductor, ensemble members, and instructors alike. It was a special moment as the selection reached its final measures. Then something changed.

As he approached the final measures of the piece "The Conductor" appeared a bit uncertain as to what he wanted to do with the baton movement and his gestures to the ensemble. He hesitated in his beat pattern as if somehow he had lost his way. Ensemble members continued to play but only in a perfunctory manner. There was little direction to the music; they were left with only the notes on the page. Everyone seemed confused with "The Conductor's" lack of involvement, and when the music ended, he simply stood on the podium, head bowed, shedding quiet tears of embarrassment in front of his ensemble.

Finally he found his words and apologized to the ensemble members. He offered no excuse; he didn't lose his place in the score; he didn't forget what he had planned for the performance. He was overwhelmed with the beauty of the music being created. He was brought to tears with the memories and feelings evoked by the exquisite sounds of Dr. Ticheli's work. He was unable to finish conducting the way he had planned; the beauty of the musical moment had rendered him without words or actions.

That special moment would never again exist in time nor could it be re-created at another time. It was unique, and the power of the beauty of it had completely engulfed "The Conductor." When he regained his composure, somewhat, he apologized to the ensemble and attempted to offer an explanation, although he still was struggling with his emotions.

He told the ensemble members, and the other graduate students and instructors, that he recently had lost his dad, and it still was an emotional time for him. He said the beauty of the piece had touched him so deeply and profoundly, the memories of his dad came back so strongly, he simply could not continue conducting as he had planned.

All he was able to do was stand on the podium when the selection was concluded and shed tears in remembrance of the wonderful times he had with his dad.

That week, the week of Father's Day, would be his first without dad, and "The Conductor" had become lost in the emotion the music had brought him. He would remember this experience for many years to come, and he would always have those wonderful memories given to him through the power of music. Music can do that, you know.

<u>**Reminder**</u>

May we never forget nor underestimate the power of emotions or feelings, and may we never forget the power of the beauty of music. Truly as Hans Christian Anderson so eloquently wrote, "Where words fail, music speaks." Once again, lesson taught; lesson learned.

"This Was <u>So</u> Special"

"I wake up to the sound of music; Mother Mary comes to me.
Speaking words of wisdom, let it be. Let it be."
— Paul McCartney

Honor band clinics come in many versions. They can vary in length, purpose, ability groupings, or design. The quality of the ensemble also is a variable that changes from year to year, depending on numbers and quality of student participation and the guest conductor invited to lead the group. In short, each honor band event is unique, despite efforts to maintain consistent enrollment numbers and musical outcomes each year. As the conductor of this particular honor band, I asked the organizers for as much background information on past bands as could be provided. It was a familiar, but still a new, challenge as I prepared for the many unknowns I would face during the three-day clinic. Always the same and always different.

I had been told to expect good players, not all-state quality necessarily, but certainly good enough to prepare a well-chosen concert. I was also informed that the most positive factor of the clinic would be the quality of the students. I would find them to be some of the best, most attentive, hard-working, and appreciative to be found anywhere in any rehearsal setting. Both were correct. It looked to be a terrific experience for the students as well as the directors in attendance.

The first rehearsal was great. We went through the process of getting acquainted, establishing some guidelines for rehearsing, working on delineating between working from a conceptional perspective rather than one which was symptomatic, establishing basic sonorities for the ensemble, and reading the tunes in the folders. Things seemed set and we headed in the right direction for a successful and special experience.

As expected, the students were delightful. They were receptive to my instructions and suggestions and our interactions as we put each musical selection together were everything I hoped they would be. Students gradually were more comfortable in responding to my questions; I even experimented with calling on some who did not readily volunteer for such things, just to make them feel more included and their opinion valued. There were no "wrong" answers to my questions; I posed them so as to allow for several degrees of "correctness." I wanted each answer to be "a version of correct." After all, this clinic experience was, in theory, something students would leave with memories of good music, possibly a better understanding of their role in the ensemble, and a better understanding of their worth as musicians. It was my responsibility to help them along this pathway.

Too many times, honor band clinics can become a forum for conductors to showcase themselves rather than one where students are the beneficiaries of their hard work. It is our duty as conductors, especially conductors of select events, to make every effort to ensure a uniquely special experience for the students we serve.

I had chosen selections for our concert which would provide an enjoyable listening experience for audience members and would be musically rewarding for the students of the ensemble. One tune in particular, William Locklear's "Wayfaring Stranger," was a favorite of the students. While technically only moderately demanding, but quite challenging musically, the students were enthralled with the wonderful interpretive things our band discovered each time we rehearsed it, not to mention the spectacular English Horn solo passages, which were beautifully played by our principal oboist. It was a perfect selection for this group of musicians.

Concert time rolled around, and the students were excited. They were pleased with the progress they had made and with the incredible musical moments we had shared over the past three days. This one had all the makings of something special for all involved and I could not have been more pleased with the work they had done and with their musical and artistic growth. All but one of the "boxes to be checked" for a successful honor band clinic had been marked. The last one was the demonstration of those things for our audience...our concert.

The final box was checked and the students were rewarded for their performance with a long and enthusiastic ovation from the appreciative audience. My students were ecstatic! As they left the stage, they congratulated each other with handshakes, high-fives, hugs, and "thumbs-up." Their hard work was appropriately recognized; it was a very good day for them. Each would take with them stories and experiences they would share with others, hopefully experiences that would make them better band members and better individuals.

I was standing near the side of the stage in order to congratulate and thank students individually as they exited the performance area. There was a line of those delightful young musicians waiting to speak with me, some even asking me to sign their program as a souvenir of the weekend. Others offered a handshake or a warm embrace. We began as strangers three days earlier; now we shared beautiful musical moments we always would have. But one of the students lingered at the back of the line as if waiting for others to leave. Sure enough, she was waiting so she could share something with me.

When it was her turn to speak to me, the only thing she was able to say before collapsing into tears was, "This was <u>so</u> special." She attempted to say more, but her words were jumbled in her tears of happiness. I heard her say something along the line of, "I never knew music could be so beautiful. This concert was one of the most beautiful things I've ever heard."

After those comments there were several other attempts to tell me more, but they were incoherent because of her emotions. I told her there was no reason to say any more; I understood completely what she was trying to say. She warmly embraced me as she finally was able to speak her last words to me, "Thank you so much. I'll never forget today and our beautiful music, especially 'Wayfaring Stranger.' This was <u>so</u> special."

<u>Reminder</u>

We have students in our classes and people in our lives who have few opportunities to experience beauty in their lives. The work we do and the music we create can bring beautiful things into the lives of the students we serve and to those whose lives intersect with ours...many times without our knowing. May we never overlook that beauty and may we always look for it at every opportunity.

"Music touches us emotionally, where words alone can't."
— Johnny Depp

The Concert For One

*"And those who were seen dancing were thought to be insane by
those who could not hear the music"*
— Friedrich Nietzsche

The young man was not a very good clarinet player, but he was a
wonderful band member. This was the kid who showed up early for
rehearsal and asked if there were things he could do to help get ready.
He was the one who hung around the band room after everyone else
had left after practice...again, just checking to see if I needed his help
with things. He volunteered to tighten music stands that had become
"wobbly," return chairs to our rehearsal set-up arrangement, file music,
even run the vacuum cleaner over the carpet in our rehearsal
room...anything except practicing his clarinet. Certainly all the things
he offered to do needed doing, but there was a definite need also for
him to spend time with his clarinet, getting better acquainted with the
finer points of tone production and technique development. Anything
to avoid dealing with the challenges of his clarinet playing.

All of us probably have had this young man in our class, only by a
different name...but very likely he was there. He was the one in my
band who would come by my office after a rehearsal to say how much
he enjoyed the pieces we were rehearsing or just to tell me "Have a
great day," as he headed to his next class. At the time, and at times, I
thought some of his actions a bit of a nuisance, but after the passing of
years and upon considerable reflection, I more fully appreciate his love
of being in the band and simply being in the band environment. He had
found something that brought pleasure and happiness to his life. Many
spend years searching for those; some never find them. The fortunate
ones do. This young man found his in the band.

One of the selections we were rehearsing and one with which the young
man was completely enthralled was Alfred Reed's "Armenian Dances,
Part One." When rehearsal ended after the first reading of the piece, the
young man could hardly wait for the after-rehearsal "crowd" to clear
so he could come to my office to tell me how much he liked the piece
and to thank me for choosing it for our band. I responded with
appropriate politeness to his compliments and told him to make sure he
practiced his part (3rd clarinet) so he could perform it well. I told him
we needed that 3rd clarinet part to be ready! I thought this would be the

end of a somewhat short-lived love affair with the piece of music, especially when he became deeply involved with learning the tricky rhythms and challenging technical passages. Once again, I mis-read the message.

One day during lunch break (band directors don't eat lunch in the school cafeteria; lunch break is one of the few times during the day when students or other faculty usually are not around) while I was in my office doing my best to catch up on paper work or possibly even spend a few minutes with scores of the pieces we were rehearsing, in walked the young man/3rd-clarinet-part specialist. He was skipping his lunch break to come to the band room. I prepared myself for a visit from him, one which undoubtedly would have a number of suggestions and questions I really would rather not answer. I just wanted to eat my sandwich, drink my cup of coffee, and get a little office work done.

Rather than head to my office for further unsolicited conversation with me, the young man went to the instrument storage room, got his clarinet, came back, went to the seat where he sat during rehearsals, took out his music, and started practicing his part to Armenian Dances. I was more than intrigued; I was captivated. This one was going to be an interesting lunch.

I watched the young man as he took the music out of the folder and placed it on the stand. He sat for a few seconds as if waiting for a downbeat, then he started playing. He would play a few measures until he came to some measures of rest, then he would sit and count until time for him to play again. Not fully understanding what was happening, I simply watched and listened. The real tests would be the mixed meter section and the technically demanding finale.

When the mixed-meter challenge arrived, he followed the same actions as before: play until there were rests, count the measure rests, then return to playing his part. I watched him in the mixed-meter section as he played, but more so as he was counting rests. During those times of counting, he would move his hand as if conducting or move his body in time with the rhythms of the dance. What was going on? I thought he was just practicing his part. What were all these other things taking place? Then, as I stood there, sandwich half-eaten, coffee getting cold, I realized what this young man was doing and what he was experiencing. I didn't say anything or interfere in any way; I didn't want to spoil the magic of the moment.

This young man of average clarinet playing abilities, one of uncommon enthusiasm for being in the band and helping "do things" for the band...this young man was involved in his "Concert For One." In his mind, he could hear the music as he sat there and played along on his part as best he could. He heard music I couldn't hear. He moved to the dance of the mixed-meter, and I could only watch. He moved his fingers over the keys of his clarinet in a frenetic fashion as he played the notes of the final Furioso section, some of which were correct, and he finished the piece with a grand cut-off of the final chord. His solo concert was a success! He had heard it and had been part of it.

I stood and watched in amazement. Sandwich forgotten and lying on my desk, coffee room temperature, I was thrilled for this young man. He never would be a great player on his instrument...but he always would be a great lover of music. The excitement he felt and the beauty he experienced were his...and his alone. I promised myself, as I stood in my office and watched his solo concert, that I would never forget the possibility of one of my band members finding beauty in places I never would look. I was excited for him, thrilled for him...and honored that I could witness this special moment in his life.

Once again, the beauty of music had called to this young man in ways I did not understand. His "Concert For One" reminded me never to stop listening for the "music I could not hear." Thank you, young man. Bravo! I thoroughly enjoyed your concert.

"Music expresses that which cannot be said and on which it is impossible to be silent."
— Victor Hugo

Luigi and The Veteran

"Where words fail, music speaks."
— Hans Christian Andersen

It was one of those all-county honor events in the early 1990s where selected students from bands, orchestras, and choirs were brought together for a couple of days of special rehearsals in preparation for a grand finale concert featuring all the honor ensembles. During the final evening a series of concerts would spotlight high school and middle school ensembles individually, each with a guest conductor. The concert site was the municipal arena, the only facility large enough to accommodate the several hundred musicians who would perform, plus the thousand or more parents and other audience members who would be present. It would be an evening filled with great music and happy people.

I had the privilege of serving as conductor of the all-county high school honor band and our performance would be the final one of the evening, the culmination of the celebration of music students and teachers in the county. The instrumental ensembles, middle and high school bands and orchestras, were seated on the floor of the arena while the large high school and middle school choirs were in the auditorium seats across from and facing the audience. The other half of the arena was reserved for audience members and, because this city in Florida was home to many retirees who loved attending concerts, those numbers could easily reach a thousand...possibly more. Family members, friends, neighbors, or those simply looking for an enjoyable way to spend an evening by attending a concert showed up for the yearly event. It was a "packed house."

Each concert proceeded as expected, well prepared and well presented. Respective conductors had chosen literature that challenged the students but rewarded them artistically and aesthetically. The order of concert performances for middle school was band, orchestra, choir; concert order for the high school ensembles was orchestra, choir, band. My band was given the honor of bringing the evening to a close, an honor not to be taken lightly.

The final selection my band would perform was Luigi Zaninelli's magnificent setting of "The Star-Spangled Banner." From our first reading of the work, students were enthralled with the harmonies and rich sonorities of the selection. They were intrigued with Mr. Zaninelli's counterpoint devices and his beautiful treatment of the original melody, especially with his inclusion of "America the Beautiful" as an added element of compositional brilliance. Our performance of this work was going to be a spectacular finale for the huge, musical celebration and our students were excited to be part of something this special.

The emcee for the evening did a masterful job of introducing each ensemble, its conductor, some background on both, and the selections to be performed. When introducing the Zaninelli work and giving a bit of background on it, he explained to the audience that, since this was a concert setting of John Stafford Smith's original composition and not the "official" National Anthem of our country, the audience could remain seated for the performance. Mr. Zaninelli wrote this beautiful work in honor of those who perished in the terrible battle of Anzio during World War II and requested that every performance of this somber and powerful work be dedicated to those who had fallen there so many years before.

The huge concert arena was completely silent as we began the piece. It was as if audience members understood the significance of this work and each found something in it to which they could relate...something upon which they could reflect. The audience remained silent...reverent almost, in respect for those lost. As we neared the end of the second verse of the selection, I noticed students in my ensemble, those not playing, beginning to glance at the audience. Members of other ensembles were doing the same. Fortunately the members of my ensemble maintained concert decor despite quiet movement in the audience. As if on cue, members of the choirs, those seated across the arena floor from our band, began standing...silently. Next were members of the other ensembles seated near us. Then the emcee. Still no sounds other than those of Zaninelli's musical homage to those who had fallen at Anzio.

The powerful final chord was held...and held. When I released it, the applause was already at full volume. It had started before the last note ended. And it continued and continued...and continued. I was overwhelmed. The students were deeply moved; some even shed tears. They probably didn't know why they were shed, but there was no need for knowing. The beauty of the performance of Mr. Zaninelli's work brought everyone together in a spectacular moment of sharing. It was a moment no one would soon forget, and most never fully understood why or how it happened.

After the concert I asked the emcee what had taken place. He said apparently there was an elderly man, possibly himself a veteran of World War II, seated somewhere in the middle of the audience, who stood midway through the selection and placed his hand over his heart. Maybe simply to honor his country; possibly he was a veteran of that terrible time, maybe he lost friends in that war; maybe he was at Anzio long ago...or maybe it was the unspoken power and beauty of the music that led him. Whatever the case, his quiet and humble gesture encouraged others to do the same.

Soon, the entire audience was standing. No noise, no talking, not even the noise of chairs or seats being moved. Silent tribute to the thousands they did not know but to whom they owed so much. Only music, such as the masterful setting of this revered tune, has the power to speak to us in ways that give us pause and reassure us of the essence of our lives. The moments, such as those shared that special night, captured that magic. Little did the elderly gentleman know how important his gesture would be in reminding those fortunate to be present of how music can inspire through its unspoken beauty.

Many years have passed since that remarkable concert. However, I still cherish those unique moments as some of my most moving and memorable, especially those we found in the performance of Mr. Zaninelli's work. Was the performance flawless? Certainly not. Were there places where the execution could have been better? Absolutely. Did those minor "things" lessen the impact on the more than a thousand in the hall that night? Not in the least.

Who would have thought symbols sketched on a page of manuscript paper could be transformed into something that spoke to so many in such a profound way? That night something very special happened. It happened only once, existed for only a few minutes, and will never be exactly replicated...but it changed the lives of all who were present. Thank you, Luigi and Mr. Veteran, for teaching us the lesson found only in the Beauty of Music. Truly...."Magnum Mysterium."

<u>Reminder</u>

May we never forget nor underestimate the power of the beauty of music. It moves us in ways not possible otherwise; it can bring comfort and solace in times when they are absent; it can unite those who have little in common; it can give purpose and meaning to those who struggle to find them; and it can bring joy inexpressible in any other way. Simply because we might not hear a performance as "beautiful," there very well might be a student who is listening with a different set of ears...and possibly with different needs that can be met only through the unique beauty of music.

Our "ears of a critic" sometimes might cause us to miss the opportunity to address the needs of someone who is only seeking something beautiful in their life. Many times beautiful things come when least expecting them.

> *"Music . . . can name the unnamable and communicate the unknowable."*
> *— Leonard Bernstein*

<u>Lesson Take-Away:</u> Teachers can show beauty to their students. They can share it with them. They can help them create it. They can teach them how to look for it. They can help them find it and make it part of their lives. Beauty never goes away once experienced.

PART TWO:
STUDENT LESSONS
Some Things They Took With Them...

A SERMON

"I'd rather see a sermon than hear one any day.
I'd rather one should walk with me than merely tell the way.
The eye's a better pupil and more willing than the ear.
Fine counsel is confusing, but example's always clear..."
— Edgar Guest

What Was It You Heard Me Say?

"I've learned that people will forget what you said, people will forget what you did, but people will never forget how you made them feel."
— *attributed to Maya Angelou*

Teachers in general never quite know what students hear or understand when instructions are given. That conundrum is even greater when one is working with band students and expecting specific results affecting the group. An additional part of this dilemma occurs long after classes are over, possibly even after the formal education process has been completed, when former students are asked what they remember and what lessons they took from their time and experiences as a member of the band. Such was the challenge I faced.

I requested from a broad and varied population of my former band students some of their thoughts and memories of lessons taken from our time together. I received responses from students who were in my classes from the first years of my career, and I received them from students who were in my ensemble at the end of my formal teaching career almost a half century later. I did not ask for nor seek personal accolades; in fact I discouraged sending them. I asked only for them to share lessons they took with them from their time in band, assuring them the information would be used anonymously and only as examples of things remembered from their time in band with me.

Here are a few "Take Away Lessons" of former students. No names are given and no identifying elements are intentionally included. Some responses were edited and, in some cases, paraphrased due only to the length or format of the replies.

Responses vary from general comments and practices to very personal statements. There are common themes to be found in many of the comments, but there are also unique perspectives in some. All are important; all are things which were taught...some intended, some as part of life's instruction...but for certain all are part of my career version of the "provenance of a rose."

I am humbled by these remembrances as they brought back many wonderful memories. Every student is a story waiting to be told, and here are excerpts from some of theirs:

****

Student Lesson #1

"It was December 1979, and our band was scheduled to perform at the Midwest International Band and Orchestra Conference in Chicago. Our concert was on a Friday evening in the Grand Ballroom of the Conrad Hilton where we had a standing-room-only audience. Our Symphonic Band was prepared and ready to perform for an audience of thousands of music educators, performers, and some of the nation's most famous conductors.

One selection in our concert was 'Ye Banks and Braes O' Bonnie Doon' by Percy Grainger, and our guest conductor was the legendary Dr. James Neilson. What came next was not in the lesson plans! As he began conducting, Dr. Neilson had a somber and humble look on his face, but at the same time, he appeared to be thankful to be making beautiful music with us. Before the selection concluded, he became quite emotional, tears were in his eyes, as we played that beautiful melody and those incomparable harmonies. Needless to say some of the band members felt just as emotional and shared tears with him.

When we finished and the silence had disappeared, the audience immediately rose to their feet and awarded the performance with a long, standing ovation...in the middle of our concert! A standing ovation was a very rare occurrence for any concert in those days, but virtually unheard of in the middle of a program.

It was then that I realized how music can move a human being through pure emotion, praise, and joy. It was then I decided I wanted to be a Band Director, just like my mentor, David Gregory. Sir, you changed my life and I will always love you for this."

****

Student Lesson #2

"The main lesson I apply to this day is: 'Sprinkle a little glitter everywhere you go,' a phrase he used when rehearsing his adult band, of which I was a member. He reminded us of the gift of music and of the joy it can bring to a person. He said joy was like glitter: beautiful wherever it landed and it stayed a long time. It stayed with whoever it touched. Music is like glitter, so he told us to 'Sprinkle a little wherever you go. It stays a long time and won't go away easily.'

I also learned that hard work, planning well, and dedication lead to success. *'Anyone can be mediocre'* was a phrase of his I have repeated countless times. Also from the years in Dr. Gregory's band I learned about teamwork, unselfishness, working hard for a goal, and then seeing that goal realized. I learned about fairness based on talent and hard work as Dr. Gregory was the first band director in our school district to have a female percussion section leader. He fought for blind auditions in District Honor Bands and All State Bands so everyone could have a fair chance based on talent alone.

One additional thing I will say. I would have dropped out of high school if not for our band program and the lifelong friends I made there. I was bullied in school, but when I was in our band room, I believed I could endure and do anything. You'll never truly know the influence band had and still has on my life."

****

Student Lesson #3

"You once said, 'I will never apologize for demanding excellence.' I have used that phrase numerous times in my life, from telling my staff what I expect of them to the kids I coached on the soccer field. 'If you give me your absolute best, then I cannot ask for anything more. Then, no matter what, I cannot be upset with the outcome of what we do together.'"

****

Student Lesson #4

"To those who understand, no explanation is needed.
To those who do not, no explanation will suffice."

"When I first started teaching, I'm not sure I truly understood what that phrase meant—or maybe I thought I did. Fresh out of college, I carried a long list of ideas about what teaching (and life) would look like: innovative lesson plans, inspired students, and endless enthusiasm. My notebook was full of hopes, strategies, and dreams for the classroom I imagined. But reality has a way of arriving quickly, and it didn't take long for those tidy expectations to meet the beautiful, messy truth of actual teaching.

The longer I teach music, the more I realize life is basically one long rehearsal. You show up, you warm up, you hit some wrong notes, you laugh about it, and—if you're lucky—you get to make something that feels like magic for about twelve seconds before the bell rings. And somewhere in the middle of it all, this phrase has followed me around like a melody that keeps popping up in different keys:

> *'To those who understand, no explanation is needed.*
> *To those who do not, no explanation will suffice.'*

Dr. Gregory's phrase has a way of popping into my mind in all kinds of situations. I've found myself saying it hundreds of times—to students, parents, and colleagues alike. When I first heard it, I thought it sounded fancy and deep—something you'd put on a mug in a calligraphy font. But after a few years of teaching, I finally understood what it meant.

Here's the thing: being a music educator is not glamorous. My mornings start with coffee that tastes vaguely of panic, and my afternoons end with picking up sheet music and lyric sheets from the chorus room floor, sheets that seemed to have multiplied like rabbits during classes. My students are wonderful chaos wrapped in vocal-program hoodies. One minute, they're debating who has the best belt in the school, and the next, they're singing Do-Re-Me off-key like it's the dramatic climax of a Broadway tragedy.

But every so often—between the missed entrances and the laughter—there's this moment. A student finally hits that impossible high note in a solo they've been dreading. A shy singer nails their first ensemble part, and the room erupts in applause. Someone leans over and whispers, 'Wait... I actually get this now!' and suddenly the air feels electric. Those are the "get it" moments. They don't appear in lesson plans or data reports. You can't grade them, and you definitely can't force them. But when they happen, you know it. You *feel* it. You understand...

On the flip side, the complementary phrase — 'to those who do not get it, no explanation will suffice'—captures the other side of the experience. And in music education, this could not be truer. You can talk about the magic of a music classroom all you want—how a harmony can lift spirits, how a solo can make the whole room hold its breath, how a struggling student suddenly finds their voice—but until someone has experienced it themselves, it's almost impossible to convey.

People who haven't spent hours rehearsing with teenagers, coaxing out their first confident note, or watching a roomful of singers suddenly lock into rhythm don't understand what it feels like. They may see students reading music or performing. Still, they don't see the invisible connections—the collective breath before a downbeat, the quiet pride in a successful rehearsal, the laughter and mistakes that build trust and community. You can describe it in words, but the essence, the spark of joy and discovery, can't truly be captured.

And that's why we, as music educators, keep sharing it. We teach not just notes and rhythms, but how to *listen*, how to *feel*, how to *be part of something bigger than ourselves*. Every rehearsal, every performance, every informal jam session is an opportunity to pass along that magic, even if it can't be fully explained. We spread it in small moments—a nod of encouragement, a patient correction, a shared laugh over a missed cue. Over time, students begin to *get it* for themselves, and that's when the phrase truly comes alive.

In this way, our work isn't just about music; it's about creating experiences that words alone cannot capture. The moments are captured in the memories and hearts of all we have the honor of having in our programs. The magic of a music classroom is a kind of secret language. It can't be explained; it can only be lived, and it keeps growing as we share it with new generations of students."

****

Student Lesson #5

"David Gregory was an amazing influence on my life even though he was my assigned public-school teacher for only one year. Here we are, some forty years later, and I still quote 'Tuning is a process and not an event.' Frankly, Dr. Gregory taught me that all music is a process each time an ensemble gathers, from intonation to blend and from tone to musical expression, with no two products being identical. Now, whether those words ever came from his mouth or whether it was simply demonstrated each time he took the podium, I could not tell you for sure. Dr. Gregory's interconnectivity of the 'process' and each

106

musical element has shaped the way I view music, teaching, and life itself.

What I remember most about Dr. Gregory are the life lessons he taught me. He was the first teacher I ever had with an earned doctorate, back when that accomplishment was far less common. In many ways, he became my earliest inspiration to pursue and earn a doctorate myself.

I also remember the day he called me into his office for a 'conversation.' I cannot recall what I had done wrong, but I'll never forget how I felt walking out. In just five minutes, he managed to let me know how deeply disappointed he was, break me down, and then build me back up to the point that I left his office feeling like a million dollars. It took me a while to realize what had actually happened and how rare that ability was. This was before anyone was talking about leadership in education or business the way they do today, but he was already practicing it in his own way.

Several years later, I returned to teach in a district where Dr. Gregory was an administrator. Everyone has experiences and conversations in their lives that leave lasting marks. One of mine was with Dr. Gregory. We were having lunch at a hole-in-the-wall diner in the county seat. I was bemoaning something that I no longer remember, which, in hindsight, shows it probably did not really matter much. (Life lesson: many of the problems over which we stress today will be forgotten in a few days or weeks). After patiently listening to me, Dr. Gregory imparted the following insight, and I will never forget it. 'There are three types of problems in this world,' he said: 'The kind of problem you can resolve, the kind of problem that will resolve itself, and the kind you cannot resolve. I would concentrate on the first type of problem.' His wisdom changed the way I looked at problems and much of life.

Rereading what I have written here reminds me of another key attribute of a great leader: they listen. Dr. Gregory not only listened but did so intently. He showed that he cared and that is why he has directly impacted countless thousands over his prestigious career."

****

Student Lesson #6

"Our middle school director was a saint. He was the perfect blend of babysitter and music teacher, and most of us loved our first band experience. There was no question I wanted to continue in band in high school. Most of my friends wanted to stay in the band too, so when I arrived on the first day of band camp, I wasn't alone. But I was a bit overwhelmed by the upperclassmen who were driving real cars and going on real dates. Things weren't perfect, but it was quickly obvious that almost everyone in the band was there to support each other.

More importantly, we weren't there just to pat each other on the back and tell each other we were doing great work. We were there to actually do good work, and this was suggested, no, demanded, by our director, David Gregory. It started with our rehearsal schedule.

Before summer band camp, I received a letter (US Mail, of course), letting me know the times and dates for the week-and-a-half camp. I remember the wording of the final sentence exactly: 'If you have conflicts for any of the rehearsals, let me know as soon as possible so we can plan for a replacement for your position.' I suspect an email sent to students from most directors in 2025, would read something like this: 'If you have conflicts for any of the rehearsals, please shoot one of my assistants a text so we won't be worried about you.' It was clear from the first communication that we were expected to be at rehearsals - not just be there, not just be on time, but be there early with instrument out, warmed up, and ready for the baton to drop at the designated rehearsal time.

When school started, we had rehearsals three times a day - 8 a.m. concert rehearsal before school, rehearsal during the school day, and marching band practice after school. That habit of being on time is something that stuck with me for the next 50 years. Luckily, my wife was in the band with me at the same time, so I don't have to worry about being late for anything.

Our marching band was good. Very good. We represented the State of Georgia in the National Bicentennial Band Contest in Allentown, PA, a contest for bands from each of the thirteen original colonies. On the night of our field performance just before our performance time, it started raining. No, the heavens opened, heavy rains came down, all of us were soaked, and the grass field was covered with an inch of water.

Band parents were whispering in our director's ear that we shouldn't march as that would put us at a disadvantage since other performances were not during a rainstorm. Dr. Gregory turned to the band and said 'What do you think? Should we do this? Do you want to march?' The band cheered in unison to take the field. We actually believed we had something to do with the decision to march. And our spectacular performance in those miserable conditions was rewarded by our band being named national marching champions of that contest!

While the band excelled at marching, I learned later that Dr. Gregory saw it as something completely different from our symphonic band work. We would have a fun concert at Christmas, always culminating with the obligatory horse whinny in Sleigh Ride. Then in January, we would gear up for the yearly GMEA Festival preparation. This event was our chance to perform three concert selections and be evaluated by highly qualified judges who were acquainted with the literature we performed. We would spend several weeks preparing those three pieces.

The students might have been pleased with just pushing the right buttons at the right time, and sometimes that was a challenge, but that was just the starting place for Dr. Gregory. We would spend the weeks working on tone, pitch, dynamics and, most importantly, listening across the band to fellow band members. The listening part was huge, because it wasn't just about me doing everything right on my own. It was about me doing my part 'in concert' with the other players.

That dependence on others for the end result was so much more fulfilling than just having a bunch of great players doing their own thing. Being in that band taught me to be on time, work hard, depend on others, and in everything I do, strive for excellence."

****

Student Lesson #7

"My freshman year in high school in 1971 was not a pleasant one for most of my class or for me. It was the first year of integration in our school system and I, along with many of my classmates, was bused to a neighborhood most of us knew nothing about. I had performed with the band during my middle school years and could walk to and from rehearsals, unlike my new school which was a twenty-minute drive.

At my new school I knew nothing about the band students or the director. I actually feared trying out once I heard them. Their instruments were so shiny and the sounds were beautiful. I decided I was not good enough to play with them but I would audition anyway. The summer of my sophomore year changed that. I felt something was missing by not participating in the band.

I was ready for rejection during that first tryout for a young director of average height and a Southern accent. My first thought was, how could such a person control a roomful of high schoolers? But he was patient with us as we tried out in small groups. He actually listened to me as I played. I gave the tryout my best shot but decided band probably would not be part of my life in high school as I didn't believe my audition went very well. I was stunned when I was accepted. I was not in the top group of players by any means, nor had I expected to be. I just wanted to be a part of something that gave me purpose. I wasn't disappointed.

Rehearsals were magical with sounds that touched every nerve in my body. I had found my home. Outside the band room high school life was difficult. Tensions between Black and White students and teachers were almost unbearable. In band rehearsals, none of that mattered and misbehavior was not tolerated. I was in a safe place. The only thing that mattered was the music.

I felt like quitting many times because of the difficulty in getting to early rehearsals, reading music on a level I had not experienced, and tolerating parents who did not support my decision to participate in this extracurricular activity. I stayed because of the music and because of the dedication I saw in the man on the podium...David Gregory. When he conducted, he seemed to be carried away by the music, and he took us with him. It was a very special time in my life.

I never played in an ensemble after high school. College and life called me in other directions. My college did not have a band but did have a chorus and I sang in it. I was blessed to hear once again what rehearsals and dedication can do with music. Thank you for caring about someone who was invisible for most of her life. The lesson I learned from you was that one person truly can make a difference to another. I try to remember that during my day-to-day interactions."

****

Student Lesson #8

"My freshman year at Hardaway High School, our band was chosen as the Bicentennial Band for the state of Georgia and we participated in the National Bicentennial Band Contest in Allentown, Pennsylvania. During my four years at Hardaway we received invitations to perform at the Midwest International Band and Orchestra Clinic, the Georgia Music Educators Association State Inservice Conference, and the American Bandmasters Association National Convention.

The thing I remember the most about David Gregory happened at the end of my sophomore year. In the late spring of my that year, he called me into his office. Thinking I had done something wrong, I was not really excited about the meeting. We sat and talked for a few minutes, and then we got down to business. He said, 'You should be doing more in this band program.' I was sitting in the middle of the trumpet section in the 2nd band and was unlikely to make the Symphonic Band the following year.

He told me he needed a good tuba player for the next year. He said he was pretty sure that with my current skill sets and musical training, I was the person to do this. At first, the transition from trumpet to tuba was difficult, but within a few weeks, everything was going well. I had hopes of doing more for the band in my new position.

The following fall when marching band season started, I was playing sousaphone. I was placed in the Symphonic band as the last chair tuba player since I was the new guy. After fall auditions I was seated as first chair tuba. Finally, I was contributing 'more' to my band as Mr. Gregory had asked of me the year before. I auditioned for All-State band and finished as an alternate that year, but I made the Georgia All-State Band my senior year. I would never have achieved this honor on the trumpet. It was only because someone had confidence in me and saw potential I wasn't using. All-State Band was a long way from the 2nd trumpet section in the second band.

I went to college and earned undergraduate and graduate degrees in music. I have continued playing tuba and trombone over the years and am retired in Denton, TX, where I still play in a community band, two big jazz bands, a jazz combo, a brass quintet, and a Dixieland combo. Without David Gregory seeing my potential at the end of my

Sophomore year and pushing me in the right direction, my life would not be the same as it is today."

****

Student Lesson #9

"I was a student in the Hardaway High School symphonic and marching bands where I played flute and was a member of the percussion section and the color guard. I learned the value of hard work, consistency, and excellence in my first year. It took me a year to earn a place in the top band. I practiced, got private lessons, and was motivated by the expectation that I could succeed.

My family moved the summer after my freshman year, and I was no longer zoned to attend Hardaway High School. I was devastated. My parents petitioned the school board to allow me to return to Hardaway and on the second appeal, they granted me permission!

Unfortunately, when my appeal was approved, summer band camp had already started, and assignments had been made, but Mr. Gregory found a place for me in the percussion section! This small flute player joined a high-intensity drum line that bolstered football games and led the annual Christmas parade! I made the Symphonic Band that year and even though I was the 'last chair' player, I was thrilled. Mr. Gregory motivated us all with his gentle spirit but fierce expectations.

During my junior year, I auditioned for and made the Color Guard in the marching band! It was a dream come true and was my favorite year in high school band. Mr. Gregory believed every person was important and each veteran member was charged with leading and helping train the newest band members.

I learned to be a leader. I learned the value of commitment and hard work. I believed I could be better at all aspects of my life. I made better grades. I had good friends and being in the band grounded me and possibly kept me out of trouble! Being in the band provided a sense of belonging that cannot be explained adequately.

After high school I continued to play flute for enjoyment at my church for many years. Band holds amazing memories for me and I believe it shaped me into the person I am today!"

****

Student Lesson #10

"Some rehearsal lessons I took with me from my years of work with"
— Dr. David Gregory:

"When rehearsing music, never waste an opportunity to work transitions, as they are typically some of the most challenging sections in any selection. (Note: Dr. Gregory reminded us parenthetically that 'transitions' in life also are some of the most difficult times.)

One of the more underrated tasks we have as band directors is to pick the 'right' music for our students. There is no substitute for quality literature. While not every band can play Holst or Grainger well, do not let that prevent you from choosing music that finds a balance between being appropriately challenging and enjoyable for the members as well as enjoyable for the audience members.

If your students do not particularly enjoy playing marches, possibly because they don't understand that style of composition...play more of them and teach them that style. Marches are notoriously challenging due to the number of simultaneous concepts required of the performer. I have even found ways to incorporate march-style exercises into our band's warmup sequence. But do not shy away from performing marches. My university band, under Dr. Gregory's direction, programmed at least one march on every concert, with very few exceptions.

Be sure to acknowledge the good effort put forth by your students, even if the results are not yet up to your standards and expectations. Students will continue to work hard as long as they know you recognize the effort they are putting into improving and are appreciative of their work."

****

Student Lesson #11

"Where to begin? My membership and involvement in the Hardaway band program were a unique experience for me, as I am sure they were for many other students. It is, without doubt, the most impactful endeavor over those high school years, perhaps even my lifetime. The lessons I learned over the course of those years have carried over throughout my adult life.

Having played the piano since a very young age, I already knew a bit about music by the time I reached high school, but the band program greatly developed and enhanced that knowledge: skills such as reading music, following the rhythm of the conductor, music theory and appreciation.

Beyond those specific areas, though, were the life lessons that have an even greater and long-lasting influence on my life and character. Discipline, commitment, perseverance, teamwork and the rewards of hard work. The band program, learned and practiced in both the marching band and the concert band, instilled those values in a young adult in far deeper ways than any other experience.

David Gregory, of course, was the leader and inspiration for all of the above. For myself, and hundreds of other young students, his influence has been one of the deepest and most enduring of anyone in my life outside of my own family. He demanded - and demanded is not too strong of a description - our best efforts and commitment ... without apology! Nothing less was worth doing. Of all the countless lessons that I learned in my band years, I'm not sure why one in particular stands out in my memory. Dr. Gregory taught us that when we put on that uniform, we were now a part of something bigger than the individual. We now represented the Hardaway High School band. And we would be held to that standard with no exceptions. And it was a very high standard.

I have gone on to live a very full and rewarding life, full of wonderful people and experiences. Ranked right among those at the top of my list are David Gregory and the Hardaway band members. Many life-long friends and wonderful memories. Hard work and expectations of the highest quality resulting in a special output of beautiful music.

These are lessons that have carried over to virtually every facet of my life over the decades since ... when I manage to live up to those standards. And the lessons that I have tried to pass down to my sons. Even with the passing of many, many years since, I continue to hold vivid memories of great appreciation and gratitude for all that David Gregory and his band program represented and instilled in myself and all of those friends around me."

****

Student Lesson #12

"I am very happy to share my very fortunate experience in having David Gregory as my teacher in Junior High and in High School. The seed for a love of music was planted in these years and continues to grow in me to this day.

In his teachings of music, he had the special talent and keen awareness of recognizing each student's strengths and weaknesses. His positive approach in teaching continued to build upon our strengths and consequently our self-esteem. He made us believe that we could achieve anything with perseverance and commitment.

If I had to give David Gregory another title, it would be: The Musical North Star! He was a gentle guiding light, leading his students to find direction and purpose and to reach their full potential. He was steadfast, unwavering and passionate in his commitment to be the best teacher to all of us. His teachings were inspiring and became my own throughline to pursue a lifelong path aligned with well-thought-out goals, values, strategies to overcome challenges, and commitment to be the best I could be in both my professional and personal life.

Upon graduating from college, I found my purpose in a very fulfilling life as a professional performer (dancer\singer\actress), teacher of dance, pediatric occupational therapist, daughter, sister, wife and grandmother. In retirement, I am a volunteer actor for student films at SCAD in Savannah, GA. I participate in various other professional acting endeavors and enjoy my studies of painting. And of course, I listen to beautiful music while I paint!

It is true that a great teacher inspires greatness and lifelong learning. Thank you, David Gregory, for your continued inspiration. I continue to find my purpose in a wonderful life."

****

Student Lesson #13

"Most of the memories that stand out to me seem to tie together. To build a successful band program, we had to be dedicated to the process and perform as we had practiced. However, if we were going to make a mistake (which can happen), then we should do it with confidence. We also heard that the worst thing in life is to be stuck in the **'quagmire**

115

of mediocrity.' Being put on the spot and holding ourselves accountable for the greater good became everyday events.

I noticed these thoughts and experiences were so ingrained in me they often came to mind when I was facing challenging situations later in life. As a result, I had the determination to complete a PhD program in mathematics, climb the academic ladder as a university professor, and take on leadership responsibilities during my career. Based on my band involvement, I found I was able to bring together individuals from diverse backgrounds to build successful programs that had a positive impact on our campus and in our community.

My participation in the Hardaway High School band program also marked the first time I had to consistently put my own plans and priorities on the back burner. I learned to give up my time for something bigger. This was especially true in the Fall each year when almost every weekend involved playing at football games, traveling to band festivals, or hosting our own festival.

Throughout the school year, we had practice before school and after school. The funny thing is that I don't remember having any trouble getting all my assignments completed for school, not having enough time to practice my instrument on my own at home, or being late for any other commitments. Whether I knew it or not, I learned time management along the way, and I no longer depended as much on my parents. I also lost any inclination I may have had toward procrastination.

Other thoughts include learning the importance of maintaining a high level of preparation after dealing with the disappointment of moving down a chair (after making first chair as a freshman) and learning to get out of my comfort zone by playing solos. These experiences served me well in my career when it came to the public speaking aspects of my job, as well as in my personal life through my participation in tennis leagues and golf tournaments."

****

Student Lesson #14

"Lessons learned during my band experience have been vital to my happiness and well-being throughout my life!

116

The discipline, hard work, sacrifice, and commitment cultivated in band have, as an adult, given me a sense of purpose and great satisfaction.

The band was my family (when my family was struggling). These relationships supported me and propped me up. I felt that I belonged. I was proud to be a member of a group that was important (at least it was important to me) and doing great things. Some of these relationships still remain substantial.

I was very lucky to have been a part of that group and will be forever grateful."

****

Student Lesson #15

"I don't have the kind of memory to tell specific occurrences, however my overall feeling and lessons of my time in band with you is: Each individual in a band, on a team, in an organization, benefits from the structure and discipline of all members so that we all accomplish more than we could have on our own.

The nature of a team (or band) is to accomplish something together. We must cooperate with each other's individual strengths and weaknesses. We pull together a bit more for someone else. We are pulled up by others. We learn to wait, to take turns, to celebrate together, and to take the blame together. We are better in many areas of our lives that serve us well for the rest of our lives.

Self-discipline, patience, humility, group project execution, group pride, and personal pride, and so much more are lessons I learned and took with me from my time in our band. I thank God for my time in high school with you as my band director.

One more...

On my walk one morning, I had another memory of a lesson I'd like to share. I remember how you would introduce a piece of music that might not have been built on a clear melody but only a melodic idea...'Pines of the Appian Way,' for example. With your narrative descriptions and body language while conducting, you helped us see it (Roman soldiers marching into that historic city on the stones of that ancient road, tombs on each side with those souls calling). We could see it and hear it as you brought this image into our story, and we also felt the victory as the music reached its climax and we held that powerful final chord. IT WAS AN INCREDIBLE EXPERIENCE! Thank you for that lesson.

Similarly, with your facial expressions and sweeping arms or very tight movements when conducting, you created yet another unforgettable experience. I find myself now, when at a concert, watching the conductor almost more than the orchestra or band members. You, as our conductor, took us on a journey using the skills developed by the members. Thanks for that!!"

****

Student Lesson #16

"My band experiences taught me skills I continued to use in my work career.

To be successful means you must work hard. You are part of a team, and what you do reflects on everyone else in the organization. In the band, you practiced, showed up on time, respected the director, pushed yourself to do things you never thought you could do, and were rewarded by the pride and respect the school showed for the band and its accomplishments.

My work life was the same. I never thought I would rise to the administrative level I did in the university system. I took pride at every level, from library assistant to Assistant VP for Business and Finance. I instilled ethics in my employees and was recognized many times by the university system for best practices. I would always remember the excitement of winning superior ratings in marching band and symphonic band competitions. I felt the same excitement with these work-related accolades.

When you are in a high school band, you are with the same people every day, working towards the same goal and building lasting friendships. Work life was the same. I would tell my staff that we are together 8-12 hours a day. I want you to be successful. In order to do that, we must work together and help each other through the challenging and stressful times. I would set the example, and I had wonderful employees who became lifelong friends, too."

****

118

Student Lesson #17

"Striving for excellence has always been a motivating factor I learned from David Gregory.

He has this ability to reach inside you and pull out the very best you have to offer. The definitions of dependability and reliability he exemplified: show up when you say you will, always be 5 minutes early, keep your promises, work hard, and do your job.

Be a leader by example. Encourage others to do their best by doing your best. Build up others; don't tear them down. Some of the life lessons I learned and continue to pursue."

****

Student Lesson #18

La Vita è Buona

"I first met Dr. Gregory when I was in high school participating in the high school band clinic at Reinhardt University. I immediately knew that I wanted to receive my music education degree there because of the way he directed bands and taught with such knowledge. I did, in fact, attend and graduate from Reinhardt with my Bachelor of Music Education degree. I also joined the Georgia Wind Symphony, an all-adult community band, when Dr. Gregory organized the group, and was one of the members who traveled with him to Italy to perform in conjunction with Alabama Winds, another adult concert band. Needless to say, this trip changed me for the better, and for good.

Travel abroad was never at the top of my to-do list as no one in my immediate family had ever been out of the country. All the stories about Italy I had heard in college from friends who had traveled there before with Dr. Gregory made me decide that if another opportunity came along to go to Italy, I would take it. The next one came in 2016. That was when I learned the phrase he so often he used with his students, 'La vita è Buona,' (Life is good), is in fact true.

A few days into our trip, the musicians from the United States joined Italian musicians for a concert in the town of Triuggio in Northern Italy. One of the selections in the concert was 'The Stars and Stripes Forever,' and I was the one assigned to play the piccolo solo that evening. To my surprise, Dr. Gregory mentioned I would be expected to stand during the solo part. If anyone knows me, they know I am on the quieter and reserved side, so to ask me to stand and play the most iconic piccolo solo in band literature...and to play it in a foreign country, was asking a lot!

I did, in fact, manage to stand during the solo, making little silly mistakes here and there due to my whole body shaking from nerves, and perform the piccolo solo of the official 'National March of the United States.' After the concert Dr. Gregory came to me and told me how proud of me he was, how he remembered my coming from a little high school in North Georgia to audition for college, and now to see me stand and play so beautifully in Italy made him very happy for me. That will always be one of the proudest moments of my life. The trip continued with incredible music, food, wine, and memories, but nothing will take the place of my piccolo solo in Italy.

The lessons Dr. Gregory taught me, and all his other 'Young Scholars,' are countless. But the one for me that encapsulates them all is 'La vita è Buona...indeed!'"

****

Student Lesson #19

"I think one of the biggest things I brought with me into my post-band life with David Gregory is the need to 'stick to it' when the going gets tough. Not only was that mindset drilled into us in terms of practicing and performing music while striving for excellence, but it was exemplified by Dr. Gregory, not just in theory but also in practice.

We often were told by him, 'If it were easy, anybody could do it.' But we weren't left to flounder alone in the difficult moments. A particularly poignant memory that exemplifies this quote has stayed with me through the years.

One spring afternoon, there was a power outage throughout the university music building. The band room had floor-to-ceiling windows on two sides so we had natural light enough to rehearse...but it was miserable: dense, stagnant air dripping with the Georgia afternoon post thunderstorm humidity in the half-light.

We all were sweating profusely as we played, but I remember no mention of quitting was made, not by the students nor by the director. I recall his suit coat and tie came off and shirt sleeves rolled up early in the rehearsal, but he kept directing and teaching. And we kept at it, pounding away, measure after measure, with only occasional pauses, during which we took the opportunity to wipe off the sweat. It didn't feel bizarre at the time; it just felt right. We had a rehearsal scheduled, so regardless of the external hindrances, the rehearsal would be held.

In that moment and during that unique rehearsal, a special and beautiful kind of music was made, albeit by sweaty musicians. Individual and ensemble character was being formed and the strength for future teaching challenges was being ingrained throughout those exhausting and trying moments.

I've thought of that rehearsal many times in circumstances of my own teaching and my own life. Remembering when we all sat, soaked with sweat, in that rehearsal room with no air conditioning and dug in and got the job done helps me face whatever situation I might encounter with the perspective: This isn't so bad; we can do this too.

Dr. Gregory could have taken the easy way out. No one would have blamed him if he had sent us home early that day (all other classes were cancelled). One lost rehearsal would soon be forgotten as the year went on. Instead, he chose to stick to it, expected us to be in it with him, and now we remember what it felt like to hang tough and not give up. It gave us a confidence and an understanding of when later trials and struggles would be faced. 'Hang tough,' he would say, 'Hang in there.' We knew he had lived it. He meant it. We knew we had lived it also, and we were capable of doing so—no matter the scenario."

****

Student Lesson #20

"There were many lessons I took with me from my years at Reinhardt University but the main one I would say is one of your sayings: 'It may have nothing to do with the music...but it has everything to do with the music.' The implication is that everything we do, everyone we meet, everything we experience, and all we encounter in our daily lives impact the way we create and share music. Our lives are reflected in our music.

Another absolutely critical lesson I took with me was that of making someone feel valued, accepted, loved...and demonstrating those traits through the sharing of your love music with others. I believe this lesson applies to people across all walks of life and in every situation.

All these jobs require knowledge of the profession, but they also require more than just knowledge itself; they call for you make a difference to others through acts of compassion, love, and kindness...traits that can make a positive impact on one's life."

****

Student Lesson #21

"I've been giving it a lot of thought on how best to sum up all the "'Lessons' I had the privilege of learning from you, and there were many. So many, in fact, I have found it difficult in some ways to summarize!

First, let me say you have been a role model for me my entire life, both directly and indirectly. I have tried with some success (and some failures) to emulate your example. Yet, no matter the result of my emulation of you, you have always stood as a beacon of excellence for me to follow, which brings me to my first 'lesson.' That is, a pursuit of excellence.

I will always remember your uncompromising demand for the best, whether in music or whatever it is one desires to pursue, give it your best, and don't settle for anything less. I have found in life there is no shame wherever you may place as long as you give it your best shot. That's all anyone can ever ask in any endeavor. Sure, first is best. Yet hard work and a clear conscience for an honest effort are more important. You taught me that, sir.

You also taught me about punctuality. I only realized it lately that you were responsible for my being such a stickler about being on time for appointments. Sometimes I drive my family nuts when I insist on leaving early enough to be on time for whatever the appointment may be! I've always thought that was important, and that's because of you.

Finally, and I believe most importantly, you have taught me to forgive myself for the mistakes I have made. I know we all make mistakes, but in my eyes, I have always been my own harshest critic. I'm sure you recall our conversation a year or two ago about my guilt for the mistakes I made as a 'dumb teenager.' I carried that guilt my whole life, and yet you showed me grace and a path to forgive myself.

122

I think of myself not as a perfect person but as a decent person. I was raised by two good parents who did the best they could in their circumstances and for that I am grateful. Outside of my family there is no doubt in my mind that YOU played the most important part in my formative years. Your example has guided me and helped give me a quality of life I would not have had otherwise, and I am eternally grateful to you.

There is so much more I could say, but I'll leave it here, sir. Thank you for all you have done for me, Dr Gregory. Your life-long student and 'Forever Young'..."

****

Student Lesson #22

"Looking back over the wonderful years I had under David Gregory's direction, I must say that one stand out take-away would be the emphasis on not being late...to anything! This timeliness carries over even to today.

He was a great music instructor in marching band, symphonic band, and jazz band and made our band exceptional in all categories. Practice! Practice! Practice! Practicing did not make us perfect, but it certainly made us our performances outstanding, even to the point of being of such high artistic levels not expected of a high school band at that time in our lives.

This way of life for us instilled in me the belief that anything worth doing is worth doing to the best of your ability. Thus, the techniques and hard work demanded from Dr Gregory carried over into my adult life and I am happy that they did. Thank you, David Gregory!"

****

Student Lesson #23

"There were a number of lessons I learned from you that have been and will always be a part of my life.

As a teacher, you saw abilities and potential in your students they did not see in themselves. I played clarinet but our band was in need of a bass clarinet player and you asked me to play that instrument also. You saw in me that ability to play the bass clarinet at a time I didn't believe

123

I could. Later in life I realized what you did as a teacher when you asked me to play another instrument was to teach me a lesson I've carried with me throughout my life...to look at the larger picture of things rather than just seeing what is in front of me. Don't always take things at face value. By the way, I still have my clarinet and my bass clarinet mouthpieces my mother bought.

Also, you taught our marching band the meaning of perseverance. You always encouraged us by telling us we '...did a good job. Now, go back and do it again. This time, find something or some way to make it even better.' This process of repetition was, and was not, just repeating the drill or routine; it was teaching us that even though we were doing good work, we always had room for improvement and still could find ways to make ourselves better. Again, you were teaching us to look at the larger picture, not just the things we saw in front of us.

From the time my Mom and Dad rented a clarinet for me and I started in the band in middle school, music was the biggest blessing of my life. Having you as my high school band director was wonderful. The lessons learned and memories made while in band will remain with me and I will cherish them for the remainder of my life. Thank you so very much for all you contributed to your students."

****

Student Lesson #24

"My interactions with Dr. David Gregory started when I was a senior in high school. I was considering two different colleges to major in music: Reinhardt University and another university in the southern part of our state. I chose the latter of the two.

I remember Dr. Gregory calling me one afternoon before I left for that university and saying to me, 'When you've finished your time at that other school, come back and be part of us at Reinhardt.' After a full year at that school, I had, in fact, finished my time there and was looking for another school. I was offered a sizable scholarship to Reinhardt and didn't have any better ideas of where to go, so I went to audition for Dr. Gregory.

While I was 'playing around' at 'that other university,' I actually did learn a great deal about playing clarinet. So when I started into my 12 major scales and 36 minor scales as was requested on the audition

124

requirements for Reinhardt, I got through about 3 majors and 9 minors and Dr. Gregory stopped me and asked, 'Are they all going to sound that good?' When I told him they would, he told me to just skip the remaining scales and proceed to the prepared pieces. After playing those for him, I don't remember exactly what he said, but I think he was happy to have me join the Wind Ensemble at Reinhardt.

After a few rehearsals playing second chair in the Wind Ensemble, our first chair clarinet player was struggling to get a small solo in one of our selections. He was absent from rehearsal one day so Dr. Gregory asked me to cover the solo...and I played it (correctly) the first time. A clarinet player seated behind me said, 'So that's how that's supposed to sound!' and Dr. Gregory followed up with, 'Well, you really threw him under the bus, didn't you?' I meant no ill will; I just played the part. This comment from Dr. Greogry and his comments during my audition had me feeling pretty good about my abilities, so I admit I had probably a little more ego than I should have had. Well, when he knows you can play, he makes you play.

Later in my years in Wind Ensemble, Dr. Gregory started adding pieces to our program like 'Molly on the Shore' and 'Capriccio Espagnol.' Demanding first clarinet parts. I spent many hours in the practice room working on these to get them to a point where I could passably play them. I was mainly trying not to embarrass myself and not let him down.

I stopped by his office one day to comment (okay, whine) about the difficulty of the parts he'd given me and he probably said something wise about dedication and perseverance. What I heard was, 'Go back to the practice room and work it out.' He had this way of giving you something you thought was too hard for you and then finding ways to help you do it. I think he knew all along I would practice, as long as it took, and I would get it right (mostly) even though I didn't think I could.

I didn't know I wanted to play difficult clarinet parts back then; they were too hard at the time. But I sure enjoy having in my collection our recording of 'Molly on the Shore' where you hear the audience clapping for the whole band and clapping even louder when he motions for me to stand. And even more, I enjoy having the memories of some wonderful musical moments in the middle of some great band and orchestra literature.

<u>**Problems 1, 2, and 3.**</u>

Dr. Gregory told us that as music education majors, we would encounter three types of problems while teaching music. The biggest challenge for us would be to figure out which problem was which, because once the problem was correctly identified, the solution came much easier.

<u>**Problem number 1**</u> is one that is solved/gets better with specific instruction. Trumpets- F sharp is second valve, not first. Clarinets - use the chromatic fingering rather than the diatonic.

<u>**Problem number 2**</u> is a like a new pair of shoes: The students are doing the correct things basically; they just need to continue to practice with correct repetitions (the new pair of shoes is the right size and style but they just need to be worn for a while before they fit well).

<u>**Problem number 3**</u> is one encountered when the students simply haven't lived long enough to develop the necessary skills. Don't try to force them into this one; this solution can come with chronological growth.

While I no longer teach music, I do often talk with my husband about his bands and I can clearly see when one of these problems pops up in some of his band stories. While I can't say these three types of problems translate flawlessly into my current profession, there are glimpses of how the general population encounter situations that fit into one of the three categories."

****

Student Lesson #25

"Just like you...

I can remember visiting Reinhardt University for my audition into the School of Music. I was graduating High School one year early with no scholarship audition slot left, only a quiet conviction that this was my school. This was the place I was meant to be. I stepped out of my aunt's car in my drumline hoodie, holding a clarinet in one hand and a voice songbook in the other. I can remember walking across the empty parking lot into the fine arts building.

When I walked into the Fine Arts building, I located an office at the end of the hall next to the band room with the door wide open. Dr.

Gregory looked up from his desk, got up, and took a step out of his office, looked at me, then at the sweatshirt, the clarinet, the book, and said, 'So… you do all of these things?'

'Y-yes, sir,' I answered, probably half-nervous and half-hopeful, and a bit confused because who is this? He smiled and said, 'Ah, I see. Well, would you like to continue doing all of those things? Because if so, you're in the right place.'

He proceeded to walk me around and show me the music building, and he let me know where I would be having my audition for the scholarships. I was a bit nervous, but I went and had my singing audition, and after that, I went for my clarinet audition. I played a solo I had performed in the eighth grade.

He started to quiz me about my selection and then he placed another piece of music in front of me and asked me to play it. Then he asked me if I would be opposed to trying the bass clarinet. I assured him that I was not opposed to it. He then says, 'Ah, this is good. See, students like you can be thrown in the deep end, and they'll swim.' We both laughed, and I replied, 'Yeah, give me anything. I'll learn how to play it. I can swim.'

That one line became the mantra that carried me through college. I swam…through every ensemble imaginable (all except two, because I literally had no more time), through lectures I wasn't even registered for, through the deep waters of curiosity and exhaustion that come with chasing every opportunity. I swam.

Dr. Gregory was what I call a teacher of permanence. His lessons didn't fade at the end of class; they lingered in how you thought, taught, and handled life. His methods weren't always traditional, but they were always intentional.

I'll never forget a mid-term exam he gave us…one filled with real-world classroom scenarios. 'Choose three of these five scenarios and respond to them in a narrative of, "How I would handle this situation."' he instructed. We wrote our most professional, well-crafted, budding, passionate young-teacher answers. Then during the follow-up meeting after the exam came the curveballs: 'What if the student says this? What if the parents react that way? What if you're the only adult they trust? What if administrators don't support this?'

That test was one of the hardest I've ever taken, because it taught a truth that no textbook could, and that education isn't about right or wrong answers. It's about the process of thinking, and the humility to know that multiple truths can and will exist at once.

Somewhere along the way, I began shaping my own philosophy: teach the whole person. The academic, the emotional, the unseen, and the part that is still learning how to survive. The music will come.

As our final class of the semester was ending, he finished his remarks to us by saying, 'May you all end up with classrooms full of students just like you.'

At first, I wasn't sure if that was a blessing or a curse. Years later, I realized it was both. It made me reflect and ask myself questions such as, How did I come across as a student? I knew I was an overachiever. A perfectionist. A lot of things, honestly. But that reflection pushed me to ask myself a bigger question: 'How can I be who I needed when I was in school?'

And let me tell you something about that phrase; it took me for a ride in my teaching career. I did end up with students who were just like me, but not in the way I expected. It wasn't just about overachievers or the kids who stayed after class to practice more. My classrooms were filled with students who had lived through traumas as I had. Traumas I still hadn't faced because I didn't know how, and I didn't have examples to follow. They needed someone to believe in them. Someone to really see them. Someone to help them, truly help them. And in trying to be who I needed for them, I realized I hadn't yet learned to take care of myself. All I knew to do was work and study the pain away.

When my students came to me, even as a mandated reporter, the only things I had to offer them were tools on how to survive their current situation. Not how to rise above it. Not how to be different. Just how to make it through another day and sprinkle a little music on top if we could handle it.

For a while, I saw that phrase 'May you have students just like you,' as a curse. But over time, I came to understand it was the biggest blessing I could've received. Because every morning, as I woke up to teach the little people how to be little people, I began realizing I was learning those same lessons myself as a grown-up human being.

A lot of my former students still say, 'Miss, you saved me in sixth grade' or 'You saved me in fifth grade.' But the truth is they saved me, too. Every single one of them. We made wonderful memories, faced impossible days, and lived through moments that felt straight out of a movie. And through it all, I was told, by those who did not understand, that because my students were 'like me,' I couldn't teach them certain kinds of music. That they wouldn't be able to learn it. That they wouldn't understand. But I never saw that as true. Because what I saw were kids who could be thrown into the deep end...and still swim.

In college, you create an idea of what your teaching philosophy will be, but out in the field, you build it from scratch every single day. That's when I understood what Dr. Gregory had been teaching us all along. Great educators don't just create musicians or scholars; they teach people how to keep swimming.

So, thank you, Doc, because of you, I will forever understand the long and the short of it.

Forever and always, Dum Spiro Spero…. While I breathe, I hope."

****

Student Lesson #26

"I remember a lot of things from my time in band, but one of the things I remember most and has stayed with me over the years is the attention to detail you insisted on. Our marching band uniforms were the old-fashioned military types and our colors were red and white with gold trim. Our pants were white with a red stripe on the side of each leg, white socks, and white shoes.

Before every marching performance, we had a uniform inspection before we left the school for the show. Our officers inspected our uniforms and instruments to make sure we were ready to perform. Back then, 'tube socks' were in style, and they all had color stripes at the top of each sock, but you couldn't see the color when we marched. But you had our officers check our socks to make sure they were 'white socks, no color at the top. No tube socks.'

At first, I thought that was a silly rule, even when you explained. You said that if we were willing to cut corners with something as little as sock color, when things got difficult during performances (or later in our adult lives), it would be easier to cut corners on the big things,

129

because we had already done that with a little thing with our socks. You kept telling us that attention to little things and not cutting corners was the something that would help make us better as a band, and later better as adults.

Thank you for that lesson. Many years later, I still remind myself not to cut corners when it's easy instead of doing the job the right way, even if it is a little more trouble to do it that way."

****

Student Lesson #27

"The lessons I learned and remember from my Gregory Years in band are all interpersonal. As an awkward teenager full of angst and insecurities, the band, the band hall, and the band director bestowed upon me a sense of acceptance and belonging.

I learned there were people I could trust and there were people in whom I could confide. I remember vividly one day my senior year when I got kicked out of my calculus class for not doing my homework and, as a consequence, I had to write a paper. Not having any idea what to do, where did I go for consolation? The band hall, of course, because of my sense of security there. I was welcomed into Mr. Gregory's office (not yet Dr. Gregory), where I learned about Vitruvius, Leonardo da Vinci, and the theory that the measurement of a person's outstretched arms equals the height of that person.

I also began my journey into conflict resolution through band and learned that adults were approachable. There was a band rule that if one missed a football game performance, one could not march again for a certain period of time. I missed a game, due to being a youth group representative at a function out of town, and I was not going to be able to participate in the upcoming marching band competition.

I felt this was unfair due to the nature of the absence from the game. My only option was to go to Mr. Gregory, explain how I was feeling and why, and hope for the best. Mr. Gregory took our conversation under advisement, rescinded the rule in my instance, and I was allowed to march at the Troy State University marching band competition my senior year.

These are but two examples of the life-long lessons learned from my band years. The band years under Mr. Gregory were the best years of my teenage life. I am still friends with several people from band, not the least of whom is Dr. David Gregory. Thank you to all who helped me through those dreadful teenage years."

****

Student Lesson #28

"Dr. David Gregory has had—and continues to have—an extraordinary impact on my life, both professionally and personally. He arrived at Reinhardt University during my second year, at a time when the program felt uncertain and uninspired. Many of us were skeptical about yet another new professor stepping into the role. But from the very beginning, it was clear that Dr. Gregory was different.

He carried himself with a confidence rooted not in ego, but in deep knowledge of what we truly needed to learn. His questions often reached beyond music, prompting us to think critically, to see issues from multiple perspectives, and to grow as people as much as musicians. He shared stories from his teaching career that revealed the profound responsibility educators carry.

One that has stayed with me was about a student named Sean, who seemed to attend school only for band. Later, Dr. Gregory discovered that Sean was living in his car. Rather than responding with frustration at Sean's lack of engagement, Dr. Gregory offered compassion and support, helping to change the trajectory of that young man's life.

The lesson for us was clear: we never truly know what burdens our students carry when they walk into rehearsal. Sometimes, simply showing up is a victory. By taking the time to know students as people, we can offer sensitivity when it is needed and accountability when it is necessary. That balance—firm expectations paired with genuine care – became a hallmark of Dr. Gregory's teaching, and it is one I strive to emulate in my own classroom.

Now, after fifteen years of teaching, I see echoes of Sean's story in my own students. A young person struggling with attendance may be holding together a family shaken by illness. Another may be facing challenges invisible to the outside world. Dr. Gregory's example reminds me to ask questions, to listen, and to support my students through their struggles.

His influence extended deeply into my student teaching experience as well. At the time, our program was still developing, and processes were being refined. Dr. Gregory's guidance was steady and encouraging. He highlighted areas where I needed to improve, but always with the goal of building me up rather than tearing me down. Because I had opportunities to teach early in my undergraduate years, I was already practicing lesson planning and instruction. Dr. Gregory sharpened those skills, teaching me the importance of pacing and the necessity of detailed preparation.

Watching him lead rehearsals was transformative. Every measure, phrase, and note was accounted for – there was never a wasted moment. I remember thinking during those first rehearsals, 'This feels like an honor band clinic. There's no way he can sustain this pace.' But he did. And he still does. His relentless preparation elevated our ensemble and set a model for how rehearsals should be run. To this day, his mantra _ 'There will never be enough rehearsal time' – drives me to push myself and my students toward excellence.

Dr. Gregory also left us with memorable one-liners that continue to shape my teaching philosophy:

- *A difference is not a difference unless a difference makes a difference.*
- *Tuning is a process, not an event.*
- *There is never enough rehearsal time.*
- *Dynamics indicated in the music are not how loudly to play, but how loudly to be heard.*
- *I will never apologize for asking for your best.*

These phrases are more than clever sayings; they are guiding principles that remind me daily of the standards he set and the wisdom he imparted.

When I think of Dr. Gregory's approach to music-making and mentoring young professionals, I am reminded of legendary coaches like Nick Saban and Vince Lombardi. Like them, Dr. Gregory is a master communicator, a leader who sets and models high standards, a tireless worker, and a mentor who cares deeply for those on those around him. His influence has shaped not only my career, but also the way I view the role of a teacher: as a coach, a guide, and a steadfast supporter of students both in and beyond the classroom."

****

Student Lesson #29

"Brad Henry once said: 'A good teacher can inspire hope, ignite the imagination, and instill a love of learning.'

My time at Reinhardt University as an undergraduate music education major was full of wonderful memories, most of which involved my incredible teacher, Dr. David Gregory. As a freshman, I was eager to make an impact in every way I could but it was Dr. Gregory, rather, who made the biggest impact on me. Dr. Gregory LOVED his students. He saw greatness that was within us and he did everything in his power to ensure that not only did we achieve greatness, but also learned how WE could instill that same desire for greatness in our students.

Our lessons together were invaluable, but one of the most meaningful given to me by Dr. Gregory during my time at Reinhardt was this: **'Every day you teach, you have a chance to do something great in the life of a student.'**

Dr. Gregory's influence continues to guide me every time I step into my classroom. His passion for teaching and belief in ALL of his students taught me that true greatness lies not in personal success, but in the impact we make on others. My hope is that I can inspire my students the same way Dr. Gregory inspired me."

****

Student Lesson #30

"I think the last time I wrote something serious to you was almost 19 years ago. Back then, I was trying to thank you for allowing me to join the band my freshman year of high school—something I now know was probably considered 'late.' But we made the best of it. I worked hard, you were patient, and eventually I made progress.

I learned to play snare drum and, somewhat unexpectedly, the tuba also. In a highly competitive high school band, I became a decent snare drummer and tuba player. In college, I played snare all four years, generally lead, and tuba during concert season—sometimes baritone as well. I never thought I had great natural talent, though my band directors sometimes disagreed. Hard work can disguise what you lack naturally, and I suspect I was more of a natural tuba player than drummer. Today, I'm simply an audiophile who can build a respectable home stereo on a frugal budget.

Music was my gateway to discipline. I eventually became a strong student by applying that same discipline to mathematics, computer science, and ROTC. Still, learning to play as a teenager when many classmates already had three or four years of experience felt like a chasm. Music taught me that a chasm can be bridged—with work, patience, and support.

There is so much more I could say. I learned my rudiments as a freshman on a broken coffee table. I learned brass fingering first on a trumpet—and eventually tuba—using an old trumpet a mailman kindly gave me. And how fortunate I was to study under two Hall of Fame band directors. That kind of mentorship is rare.

What I didn't say in my earlier letter is that my family wasn't just poor—we were resource-challenged. That wasn't uncommon in the South during the 1970s. I once read a post from a former bandmate saying she didn't know anyone in the band who qualified for free or reduced lunch. I did. I just kept it to myself. I'm sure I wasn't the only one; it's just a better story when it doesn't start humbly.

After college, I worked in an applied science lab as a mathematician and computer scientist. After work, I tutored trigonometry and pre-calculus to inner-city kids in Detroit, and everywhere I moved there were students who needed help with algebra, geometry, and pre-calculus. If they made it past that, they were usually headed in the right direction. I also tutored computer science to engineering students.

One lesson music taught me is that 'not understanding' is often just a matter of lacking resources and exposure. So I've always tried to meet students where they are. I'll admit, sometimes I need breaks from that fight—but I always seem to return.

Today, I am a retired engineer and Army Lieutenant Colonel. Had you not allowed me to join the band, I'm not certain my story would have unfolded this way. I remain deeply grateful for your patience, your belief in me, and the opportunity you gave a very unpolished freshman so many years ago."

****

Student Lesson #31

"What did I learn from Dr Gregory? Luckily, I found a letter from 2014 where I communicated this very thing. To be honest, I'm not sure if I sent it or not. As I read it now, it seems pretty vulnerable, but if I didn't share it–here it is now in abbreviated form.

I don't think I could quote any exact "Gregory-isms" from our years together, although I know your wisdom left its mark on me. What does come to mind, though, is something attributed to Maya Angelou:

'I've learned that people will forget what you said, people will forget what you did, but people will never forget how you made them feel.'

And that's exactly what stands out to me when I think of you. I remember 'how you made me feel.'

When I look back on my high school years, I often ask myself what made you stand out so vividly—and the answer always comes easily. You made me feel important, significant, and most of all, cared for. I can't think of a single time when you didn't make me feel like I mattered. Even in disagreement, there was still a respect for me and my misplaced convictions.

Looking back now as an adult, I realize how rare and meaningful that was. You never made me feel like a 'typical teenager' whose opinions didn't count. You listened, you challenged me, and you expected more from me—and because of that, I saw myself as a leader when I graduated from high school.

That's why it hit so hard a couple of years later when I found myself a mediocre music major, struggling to figure out who I was and what I was doing. One of my college music professors made a passing comment—probably meant to motivate me—but it landed differently. He said he hadn't seen any leadership qualities in me and hoped I'd start showing more.

Ouch. That wasn't how I saw myself. That's not how Dr. Gregory saw me! But that moment stuck and, honestly, it planted some negative thoughts about me that took years to work through. I don't blame him—he wasn't wrong about me in that moment—but I bring it up because it reminds me just how powerful teachers' words can be. Especially music teachers, who spend years with their students and often become part of their emotional world. You helped shape how I saw myself—for the better.

And here's the best part: you inspired me to want to do the same for others. You planted a deep desire in my heart to make a difference in kids' lives. I wanted to be someone's 'David Gregory' one day—to have a student look back and say I made them feel seen and capable and valued.

And I got that chance. I ended up in education and, thanks to the example you set, I was able to impact some lives along the way. Every time I encouraged a student, every time I believed in one who didn't yet believe in themselves—I was channeling a little bit of Dr G!

In the end, you taught me something that goes far beyond music: the greatest teachers don't just share knowledge—they shape people. You showed me that making someone feel valued can change the entire trajectory of their life. Words matter and yours still hold a lot of weight in my world!"

PART THREE:
FROM THE LESSONS LEARNED...
WHAT WOULD I SAY?

To Wrap It UP...

From the lessons taught me by my students, what would I say to my profession?

I would say I am experiencing a dilemma as to what young teachers possibly perceive our profession to be, versus the essence of what it truly is. Motivation and inspiration are essential parts of our work, but the "perspiration" aspect of our work is equally important, possibly even more vital, to success and fulfillment in one's professional life as their body of work is compiled over years of application. A balanced "work diet" if you will.

Teaching is all about making decisions; teaching is a commitment; and a commitment is a decision we make every day, over and over. My dilemma stems from this premise. I fear too many choices to "become a teacher" are made as a result of the excitement of a motivational or inspirational event or events, and that is not altogether a bad thing. Excitement about teaching is always a good thing...the inspiration part. And we need those who remind us of that on a regular basis. The challenge arises, however, when the young professional is faced with the daily grind of the job...the perspiration part of the job. And we need those who remind us of that and help us successfully navigate it.

The avalanche of administrative demands, the challenge of motivating students who seem uninterested, retaining students in the program, parent and community expectations, sufficient funding for band activities, and the constant pressure "to win" or "to be competitive" seem to overwhelm the young teacher who might have thought the job was going to be more along the line of conducting good music and getting students excited about being in the band. After all, the motivational workshops the young teacher attended certainly led one to believe that to be a possibility, and participants left those clinics inspired and motivated about doing their work. As I said, not a bad thing at all.

I believe such events are in no way intended as a deception, but I feel they are received more as an incomplete message. While vitally important to the teacher, motivation alone does not address the essence of the challenges of teaching, nor does it guarantee success in the classroom. Therein lies my dilemma. What do we do about this challenge and how do we address it?

I submit that one of the first fronts to address in helping equip and retain teachers is through the college/university teacher preparation programs, knowing this statement is in itself somewhat counterintuitive. However, by way of clarification, I believe those who teach music education courses and work directly with those students should be those with proven records of successful teaching in school music programs. To do otherwise is to lessen the value of music education preparation, both through actions and non-actions. I believe only those who truly are qualified should be the ones who teach future teachers. That should be a tenet of our teacher preparation institutions.

A caveat regarding those who "teach music education classes": all who teach future music educators are, in fact, "music educators."

Somehow there is the perception that one can be "only a conductor" of a fine ensemble and not be a "music educator." Much to our professional chagrin we have allowed the title of Music Educator to become less attractive and less worthy, even to the point at times of being regarded as a less-than-top-tier position. I believe we have glamorized "conducting" over "teaching" and the titles of Wind Conductor, Director of Instrumental Activities, Ensemble Coordinator, Director of Wind Band Studies, etc. over Music Educator, to the extent we have in many cases separated "Wind Band" and "Conducting" from Music Education. And that is one of the great educational and artistic misfortunes of this generation of teachers of music.

Our profession has created a prevalence of undergraduate music students who move immediately into graduate school or spend only a few years working with school bands before retreating to academia to work toward one of the aforementioned titled positions. Possibly, we have encouraged this metamorphosis through so many "conducting workshops" that focus only on that aspect rather than including the "teaching" aspect of our podium work. We need to nurture and develop strong, dedicated school band directors who are excellent musicians and conductors and who <u>do not</u> leave the profession to pursue academia. The future of our art form lies with strong TEACHER/CONDUCTORS, not with those who aspire only to be conductors. This I believe to be true.

I submit that unless every member of the ensemble in front of which the conductor stands is preparing for a career as a performer and there are no future teachers in that ensemble, such titles might allow the conductors to separate themselves from the education process. *(Although, the person on the podium actually is engaged in "music education" through the creating and sharing of the artistic aspect of music.)* Conversely, any conductor who stands before an ensemble in which there are music education students, students who will become music teachers, is in fact a music educator who is involved in the process of music education, regardless of the chosen or preferred title.

Every rehearsal is a music education class. Every concert is a lesson is programming and concert protocol. Every hour spent in rehearsals is one spent training future teachers in classroom management skills, rehearsal techniques, problem-solving strategies, time management practices, group discipline, and the demonstration of mutual respect between conductor and ensemble. One cannot divorce oneself from the "education" aspect of conducting no matter how much one would prefer to be known only as a "conductor."

Those who have the honor and privilege of conducting top ensembles at colleges and universities must remember the responsibility they have to those who wish to follow their calling to become music teachers. They are in your ensembles to learn from you, to model after you, to take with them your rehearsal practices...to become a teacher such as you. You are their musical guide; you are their music educator. Wear that title with great honor. I would say that to my profession and to my colleagues for whom I have great respect.

In my opinion, it is not sufficient measure for a music education instructor in a teacher preparation program to bring to their classrooms only a few years of teaching experience, possibly an even more limited body of work with school bands (successful or otherwise), and a graduate degree as proof of their qualifications for preparing future middle and high school directors. Nothing substitutes for real-life classroom experiences and years of evolving and refining one's philosophy of teaching and guiding young people. One cannot teach what one does not know or has not experienced. That, I believe, is a major concern and is the root of my personal dilemma.

Without the proven validity of the university instructor's true qualifications, the music education students/future teachers will not receive sufficient classroom preparation and will be ill-equipped to face the onslaught of "real life" challenges awaiting them in the classroom. Is it any wonder young teachers soon leave the profession after attempting to survive the withering pressures and expectations in today's classrooms where the teacher many times feels there is little to no administrative support? No matter how hard they try, they cannot recapture the excitement of their first year of teaching nor can they motivate their students enough to excel. They feel hopeless...and helpless.

Such is my dilemma. I do believe, however, once a problem is clearly and succinctly stated, the solution lies within reach. But first, as a profession, we must recognize the inherent problem of the lack of realistic preparation provided in many teacher training programs and we must address that issue in clear and specific ways. Knowing the answer is the easy part; saying it out loud is the hard part.

If we truly believe what we say we believe, our actions will follow those statements. This I believe...and this is what I would say.

Closing the Book

"We are what we repeatedly do. Excellence, then, is not an act, but a habit."
— Aristotle

"If This Were My Final GMEA Clinic, What Would I Say?"

This title seemed an appropriate summary of many of the "lessons" my students, of all ages, taught me during my career as well as things I "took away" from those years. It is even more fitting that these thoughts and comments were presented at my final Georgia Music Educators Association clinic, entitled as such, in honor of them...the teachers with whom I worked and the students whom I was privileged to serve.

Those clinic comments have been modified and adapted for presentation to my profession. So...

"If This Were My Final Clinic Presentation, What Would I Say to My Profession?"

I have been given so much and been taught so many things...and because of that, what would I want to say, **if** this were my final clinic? Decades of experiences, thousands of students, and memories of so many beautiful musical moments fill my mind. I would begin with some thoughts on my profession. These reminders...some are mine; others are borrowed... have been and still are special to me:

* Be a strong advocate for your profession; publicize your own program.

* Organization cannot make your ensemble sound good; a lack of organization can prevent it from sounding good.

* Be careful how you use social media. Posted things remain.

* Never assume others know what good things are taking place in your program; you must be your own advocate.

* Parents do not grow weary of hearing good things about their children.

* Don't give up on your students, your work, or yourself.

* Look for greatness in the everyday things of your work.

* Not all are gifted on the podium. There are many, many other aspects of being a good music teacher...a good teacher of young people. Work to find your gifts...on or off the podium.

* For you to do well, others do not necessarily have to do poorly,

* Remember that there are students in your classes every day who are looking to you for guidance and inspiration...they are not interested in the inconveniences of your personal life.

* Be careful whom you choose for "role models" and "music education experts" for your programs and our profession. Those we name represent what we supposedly hold as our core values.

* Networking and connections are good and necessary for certain things; they alone do not bring about quality music programs.

* To your students, you are music. Be careful how you deliver your message and how you handle that responsibility.

* We teach many lessons to our students...some of them are things we intend to teach, others we may not even know we have taught.

* There are times, possibly many of them, you will consider giving up. Don't.

* There is no greater reward than sharing the compelling beauty of music with our students. Few professions offer such things. Be careful not to take for granted those things we have been allowed to have.

*Work diligently to keep the "stuff" of our business from obscuring and preventing us from experiencing the "essence" of our profession.

* Our students need good heroes in their lives. Be one for yours.

* If our students cannot learn the way we teach, we must teach the way they learn.

* Teaching is all about making decisions.

* It has everything to do with the person on the podium.

* You will change the lives of many of your students. There are students you teach who will change your life.

* If you truly believe what you say you believe, your actions will reflect those beliefs.

* If I had to do it all over again, I'd do it all over again.

* It goes by in a blink.

****

Ours is a noble profession. In spite of all the clichés, criticisms, complications, and broad misunderstandings of what we do, ours is one of the most admirable and worthy of professions. It is not one that should be taken lightly nor one that should be thought of or entered into as a "fallback" for other jobs that did not work out. It is one that must be protected by the wisdom of choices and guided by the determination of purpose. If it is not, I fear we all will continue to suffer changes that are not necessarily in the best interest of our profession and the students we serve. So...

If this were my final professional clinic...

What would I say as I leave? I think first and foremost, I would challenge you who will soon lead to guard and protect and guide this wonderful profession that gives so much more than it takes. One that changes the lives of students and teachers alike. One that guides the tenets and structures of our society. One unlike any other.

I would say to you, those who are inheriting this art form from those of us who are passing the torch…be good teachers. Be teachers who care about your students more than you care about your professional reputation; more about their lives than about trophies collected; more about the influence you have in helping them shape their futures than about ratings and contests; and more about how you made your students feel about music and the beauty it brings to their lives than about "being important" in our profession. Just make certain you are important in the lives of your students.

****

I would challenge you to rehearse and perform good music…**if this very likely were my final clinic**. Do not be swept away with the "composer de jour" or by peer and social media pressure. Be captured and intrigued and challenged by artistic compositions that reward effort with quality. Involve yourself in music that gives students an opportunity to experience magical and aesthetic moments that otherwise would not come into their lives. You are the one who guides your program and helps shape your students' outlook on music for the rest of their lives.

And by the way on a lighter and more humorous note, if you're over the age of 35 (possibly 30), it's probably time for "awesome" to

146

disappear from your regular professional vocabulary, especially on the podium. Awesome is used for so many things and in such diverse ways, it loses the impact of its true meaning. No longer is it...well, awesome. Find other words.

I would say that only those who are committed on a personal level and well prepared on the professional level are the ones who will be able to achieve true musical and artistic excellence. Such commitment and preparation do not come easily. A commitment is a decision made over and over, again and again...daily; preparation involves years of dedication to learning the skills necessary to move from application to artistry.

Do not give up easily in pursuing this "inner circle of excellence" in your work, or allow yourself to settle too easily for lower standards of expectations in your ensembles. Never apologize for insisting on excellence with your students. You may be one of the very few who cares enough to do so for some of those entrusted to your care. Good enough should never be good enough.

****

Since this could be my final clinic...

I would say to you... my friends, my peers, my colleagues, my profession...please stay away from social media with juvenile and self-serving postings. Please. It is quite presumptuous to assume others are interested in countless "selfies," "live happenings," or "humble brags" designed for gratuitous self-promotion, no matter under what pretense they might be presented. They are there for one main purpose: to make the person appear more important and more relevant. Anyone beyond a reasonable age, in reality any age, quite simply should not be involved in disingenuous self-honoring. Should others post something positive about or in honor of you...different story, and I hope there are many of those. But we must stop tainting and lessening the value of the work we do by engaging in self-adulation.

We supposedly are the adults in our profession. I think we, as professionals and adults, should not engage in postings and activities such as those we would expect of adolescents. Remember...the parents of our students, our professional colleagues, community members, and our students see the immature things that are often posted.

147

Think carefully about posting personal things on social media. It is not always in one's best interest to upload things regarding personal health issues, relationship problems, or comments about personal recognitions. Keep those personal things as just that…personal. However, there are times when posting health and personal scenarios could be appropriate, but only a few. Just make certain your postings, should you upload them, do not appear to be pandering for attention.

Last thing about social media postings…it seems as if this form of communication has provided a forum for much of the darker and more base and vulgar elements of our society to espouse hatred and hurtful comments. Please rise above such things. It is not in our best interests, personal or professional, to be part of the folly that seems to pervade many postings. I urge you to choose your postings carefully and thoughtfully and to rise above the negative elements so pervasive in our society. It would be good if we heeded the words of Abraham Lincoln when he spoke of "the better angels of our nature."

I urge you also to think about how we "self-promote" and how we present ourselves to others. Is it necessary that, as part of our email signatures, we list every title we have, the committees we chair, the awards we have received, or the titles we have secured? Do we really need to remind everyone of our credentials on EVERY email, no matter how formal or informal the message? How about just on official correspondence? In the words of the poet Robert Burns, "…may we have the gift to see ourselves as others see us."

****

In my final clinic, if this were it...

I would remind my younger colleagues that the surge in popularity of "conducting workshops" is something that should be examined very thoroughly. Many are workshops designed primarily to make the conductor look better on the podium; they are not rehearsal clinics designed to make your ensembles sound better.

Also, those who are the "visiting artists" for conducting workshops should be ones who have proven themselves to be successful in "performing and rehearsing/teaching" their respective ensembles, and not someone who is chosen because she/he is in a prestigious position, has written yet another book on conducting, or is espousing ideas and techniques that have little or nothing to do with teaching students.

As Dr. Harry Begian, legendary former Director of Bands at the University of Illinois, used to tell us young conductors many years ago, **"The show is not on the podium."** But I'm afraid today we are allowing ourselves to believe it is. As my dear friend Dr. Bobby Adams, former Director of Bands at Stetson University and highly successful director of high school bands in Florida for many years, used to remind us, **"If your band can't play well, it doesn't matter how great you look on the podium."**

****

I would say to you, if this were my final clinic...

You must be careful as to how you choose those whom you place in leadership, role model, and decision-making positions in our profession. I suspect there is very little evidence, if any, supporting the premise that one can serve as an effective and insightful voice of authority and guidance to music programs if that person has never had a fine program of their own. Simply because one has good administrative skills or has demonstrated expertise in another field does not necessarily qualify that person to be a musical expert. Look at what a person has done and is doing before declaring them to be a leader in our profession. Just a reminder...

****

My final clinic, if this were it...

would include my statement to my profession that I believe it is very difficult, virtually impossible, for someone who has never had a truly fine musical ensemble or conducted an artistic performance to render sound and valid adjudication insights along those lines to other programs. I believe it to be counterintuitive when one expects someone to render such comments for helping ensemble performances become "superior" when the person offering those comments never had a comparable ensemble that truly was "superior." I would not bring up these controversial topics, unless **this possibly were my final clinic.**

****

I would remind you, if this were my final clinic...

that our work is a difficult and seemingly impossible task. Were it not so, anyone could do our jobs. Difficult work demands strong and qualified professionals. Certainly, our professional obligations and

149

responsibilities are at times overwhelming…but the rewards of our work are unlike those in any other profession.

I would say to my profession, we need "a professional conscience," a voice, or voices, not afraid to speak to issues in a truthful and professional way. A professional conscience seems to be missing in much of our work today. There is a conspicuous silence much of the time, and I am saddened because of it. As a result, there are many people and many philosophies receiving accolades and endorsements from our profession…to a large extent because there are not those who will speak and say, **"But the Emperor has no clothes."** Without a voice of conscience, our profession easily can become one of great breadth but very little depth…one filled with activities and events which are little more than motivational schemes and self-aggrandizing promotions. So desperately does our profession need those voices to help guide us, and remind us, and challenge us!

There does not seem to be enough of those today who speak clearly and wisely from our college and university ranks, as there were in the past. Nor do I hear clearly the voices in our public schools that caution and advise our profession with wisdom. I fear too easily we allow ourselves to be drawn to things without due and careful consideration. I am concerned we listen too often to those who speak the loudest and with greater fanfare than we do to those who dedicate themselves more to their students and our profession than to their reputations. There are those who work hard to gain personal and professional recognitions…and then there are those who receive such recognitions because they work hard for the things that are best for their students.

I would offer a special caution to my profession regarding the slippery slope of straying from conducting and teaching and venturing into indoctrination. I posit that if our students, because of our comments and actions on the podium, know our specific political and/or religious beliefs, we have departed the realm of instruction and entered into the arena of indoctrination. The podium, a place where very few get to stand, should not be a forum for political comments, religious bias, personal prejudices, or inappropriate social commentary.

Our students do not need those distractions in rehearsals; there are too many such things in society already that attempt to attack them on a daily basis. Our podium should be a special place, a place like no other, one of teaching and challenging and helping to shape the lives of our students. We should guide through example and teach from solid pedagogical tenets. Leave indoctrination to those who are assigned that duty...not to those of who occupy the podium.

I would say to you, my colleagues, and to those who soon will carry our professional torch, you must stand strong for the ideals and values of music education and music making in our schools. You must not sell short, or allow others to do so, this unique profession and our ability to change the lives of our students with and through our love of the beauty of music and through the power of music performance.

****

If this were my final clinic session, what else would I want to say?

Those who will assume the mantle of responsibility for our profession should know you will experience some of the most profound and meaningful experiences of your life in this beautiful world of music. Do not take them for granted; always be receptive to the possibility of their happening.

Our profession has many lessons for us: Teaching is all about making decisions. If students cannot learn the way we teach, we must teach the way they learn. Good enough should never be good enough in our profession. Ours is a profession that should have as a tenet never to apologize for insisting on excellence in the work and lives of our students. Our profession reminds us that while we might believe we are teaching and instructing and guiding our students and preparing them for the future, they are, in fact, doing that for us. Truly, our lives as teachers are given special meaning because our beloved profession brings students to our classrooms who will impact and change the lives of those who serve as their teachers.

You, my fellow and future teachers, will have the opportunity to give to your students things that will enrich their lives and help make them better people through your work with them. As a result, they will in turn enrich your life in ways you never expected. May you who assume responsibility for guiding this wonderful profession also find great joy and immeasurable rewards. May you find and create your personal "Magnum Mysterium."

And since this _is_ my final clinic...

The final thing I would say to and about my profession is something that has guided me and motivated me through my years, and it is this:

Every day I went to work...every day, I had the opportunity to do something great in the life of a student. What other profession can make that statement to the extent we can? What greater challenge? What greater responsibility? In the words of the ancient poet and lyricist, "May the words of our mouth and the meditations of our heart be acceptable." And may those who carry this profession in future years always have words that are wise and acceptable, and may they never forget that every day there will be opportunities to do something great in the life of someone else.

An important part of our work, and certainly that of every clinic, is knowing when to end. As baseball's "Old Professor," New York Yankees' longtime manager Casey Stengel, once said, "There comes a time in every man's life, and I've had plenty of them." It's that time for me...time to close this "clinic" and move on. Time to hand over my part to the next generation of wonderful and talented teachers.

This profession has given me a career filled with amazing people, incredible events, and life-changing experiences. For those things I am most grateful. To those who will follow, you will have countless opportunities in this profession to find rewards and fulfillment through the students you serve and the beautiful music you create.

Words cannot sufficiently express how enormously grateful I am to have been part of a profession that can change lives so profoundly. As so beautifully phrased in the lyrics from a selection in the Broadway musical "Wicked," *"I do believe I have been changed for the better. And because I knew you, because I knew you...I have been changed for good."*

To those who follow in this beautiful world of music, know this: you will be changed...for good. Such is the provenance of our profession.

CODA

I began my clinic with some statements of gratitude and some for consideration, and I would like to close my final clinic with a few last thoughts along that same line. As before, some are mine, some are borrowed, and others are on permanent loan:

*We don't use great students to make music; we use music to make great students.

*Few get to do the things we do.

*There are few things in life more rewarding than helping to change a life in a positive way.

*There will be times you want to give up on your profession. Don't do it. If you do, there will be one less of you.

*There will be tough times that will come your way.

*Being right, caring, hard-working, helpful, professional, and student-centered will not always protect you from harsh things and hurtful people that might come into your life. Keep being those things anyway.

*There will be those whom you will influence for the rest of their lives.

*There will be those who come into your life who will influence you for the rest of your life.

*When it's all said and done and the last trophies and plaques have been handed out, and all the rankings and places declared...the only things that will remain in the lives of the student you served are: how you treated them, how you made them feel, what you helped them accomplish, and how you influenced the person they became after their time with you.

*After so many years in this splendid profession, I say to you one more time... it goes by in a blink.

*And one more time...If I had to do it all over again, I'd do it all over again.

In the beautiful words of Winnie the Pooh, "How lucky I am to have something that makes saying goodbye so hard." With that, I bid each of you and all of you...my friends, my colleagues, my mentors, my students, my heroes...my profession, a fond and affectionate farewell as I "yield the podium" to the next generation of teacher/conductors.

Because you made me a better person, you helped me make others better.

Ours is a great and noble profession. To those who are chosen, and privileged, to inherit it...guard it; guide it; protect it; enjoy it; love it; and let it make you a better person.

One Final Reminder — To My Profession, and Those Who Will Follow

John Muir, late nineteenth-century naturalist and defender of our national parks, once stated that occasionally he would go into a forest during a thunderstorm and climb to the top of a very tall tree. By doing so, he would have a better view of the magnitude of the storm as well as what was taking place around him. He also could experience first-hand some of the powerful forces to which the tree was exposed during the turmoil. I suggest that we as individuals "climb some trees" in our profession. Perhaps we will see better and more realistically some of the changes taking place...and possibly can better understand some of the struggles of our students and those around us.

There are two things we get every day when we wake up: a chance and a choice."
—Attributed to J. Prince.

"Our life and the lives of others are impacted by the choices we make and how we use the chances we are given."
—David Gregory

Epilogue

A Student Take-Away of Mine, In Honor of...

My Mentor, My Teacher, My Friend... Dr. William J. Moody

"Human nature will not flourish... if planted for too long in the same worn-out soil. My children, so far as their fortunes may be within my control, shall strike their roots in unaccustomed earth."
Nathaniel Hawthorne

My first honor band clinic experience changed my life. I am sure the social aspect of being with so many musicians from other high schools, the rehearsal and concert venue, the excitement of traveling to another place for the event, and exposure to new and challenging music...all were factors that impacted the experience. But the **conductor**. The conductor was the person who made the real difference for me. Dr. William J. Moody was that person. He entered my life that weekend and helped set me on the path to a lifetime of sharing the beauty of music with others...and he would continue to shape that path for more than half a century. Bill Moody was my first significant encounter with and encouragement to move toward my personal "unaccustomed earth."

My decision to study music and become a band director was followed by my choice to study with Dr. Moody at the University of Southern Mississippi, where he was Director of Bands. He had come to Hattiesburg, Mississippi, from Northern Minnesota in the early 1960s (much more than simply a major geographical move) to begin a career that would help change the landscape of bands in America. That move was a demonstration of <u>his</u> personal commitment to "unaccustomed earth."

While at USM, I became even more committed to my calling in music, primarily because of the influence Dr. Moody had on my life, on the way I conducted daily undertakings, and on the way I formulated my philosophy of dealing with others. It was from him that I learned that answers bring more questions, solutions suggest further investigation, problems bring about changes, persistence in the pursuit of knowledge is a worthy trait, apologies are never needed for insisting upon excellence, and doing the right and moral thing always is the goal. Yet more "unaccustomed earth."

Once my teaching career was established and I had begun to realize the impact of William Moody on my teaching philosophy, or perhaps I should say on my philosophy of life, I found myself holding his standards of musical and professional excellence as mine. There was never a concert or clinic or guest conducting appearance where I did not ask myself in some way, "Would Bill Moody be pleased with what I've done?" or "Have I taught these students well enough to meet his standards?" or "What would Bill think about this concert?"

Through his teachings and questionings and moving me out of my comfort zone, I found myself changed, or possibly I should say "changing," the longer I taught. Always his influence was felt; always I sought his approval; always I wanted to be the person/teacher he believed I could be… always finding my way onto even more "unaccustomed earth."

In addition to the mentor/mentee relationship we enjoyed for more than 50 years, Bill and I became close friends in the later years of my career, and especially in his final years. We had the opportunity to travel together to musical events and to work together as colleagues. Toward the end of his life, I was honored to have him conduct my university wind ensemble at a national convention. During his rehearsal with my students, he told them that having the privilege of conducting my band at this prestigious event was one of the greatest rewards he could have as a teacher/conductor. Even for him at this stage in life, he still was finding and appreciating "unaccustomed earth."

One of the final times the two of us were together was at his last Midwest Clinic. We had a long lunch visit, during which he reminisced about his work, his career, his students, our art form, the influence teachers have on the lives of students, and other "Moody Musings." As our visit was coming to a close, he paused and said to me in one of the most emotional and moving moments I ever experienced with him, "David, the only way I really want to be remembered is as a teacher who simply would not give up on his students." My response, "You are, Bill. That's the way we think of you. We're better at what we do because you always expected that of us. That'll always be our memory of you."

His health declined rather steadily following that Midwest Clinic, but we visited often by phone as we lived quite a distance from one another. When his medical conditions became such that Bill's final days were approaching, I made certain to call him and say some things to him I needed and wanted to say. Our final conversation was a good one, and as it was coming to an end, I said to him, "Bill, I want to thank you for all you did for me and how much you influenced my life and my career. I love you because of that." His response was, even in this final conversation with me, quintessential Moody. His question (still questioning and learning) was, "So how do you know that?" My last words to him, spoken with great affection, were, "Because you made me a better person and you helped me make others better." His response: "That's a very good answer, David. Thank you."

My mentor, my friend, my musical inspiration, the one to whom I owe so much: William J. Moody… the one who always moved me toward "unaccustomed earth."

"The dream begins, most of the time, with a teacher who believes in you" — Dan Rather

FINE

About the Author

David Gregory is a highly successful teacher of young people. More specifically, he is a band director...one who has earned the respect of and accolades from his profession through his work with elementary, middle school, high school, college, university, military, and professional musicians. His personal and professional honors and recognitions are numerous and significant, and are ones that span a career of more than five decades. He has served his profession in many appointed and elected positions, from locally appointed offices during the early years of his teaching to the election as President of the National Band Association, the world's largest band organization, later in his career.

His bands have performed for dozens of regional and national conferences; he has been featured as a keynote speaker at numerous music conferences and conventions; he has served as advisor and consultant for schools and school systems across the country; and his adjudication and conducting invitations have taken him throughout the United States, Great Britian and Western Europe. His clinic presentations are used as models for programs and teachers across the music profession.

Dr. Gregory brings to his presentations and writings a long and varied background in public school and higher education work. He has been a classroom teacher (band director), Music Supervisor, Assistant to the Superintendent of a major metropolitan school system, and Director of Bands at the university level. His professional memberships and associations, both past and present, are vast, and his conducting appearances in Europe have given him a better and broader perspective of many of the critical issues facing teachers and students today.

His insights into "Lessons" taught by students serve as sources of inspiration, motivation, understanding, discovery, and humor for teachers, as well as others who are not "professional educators." As he states, "At times, each of us is a teacher and each of us a student. We learn as both."